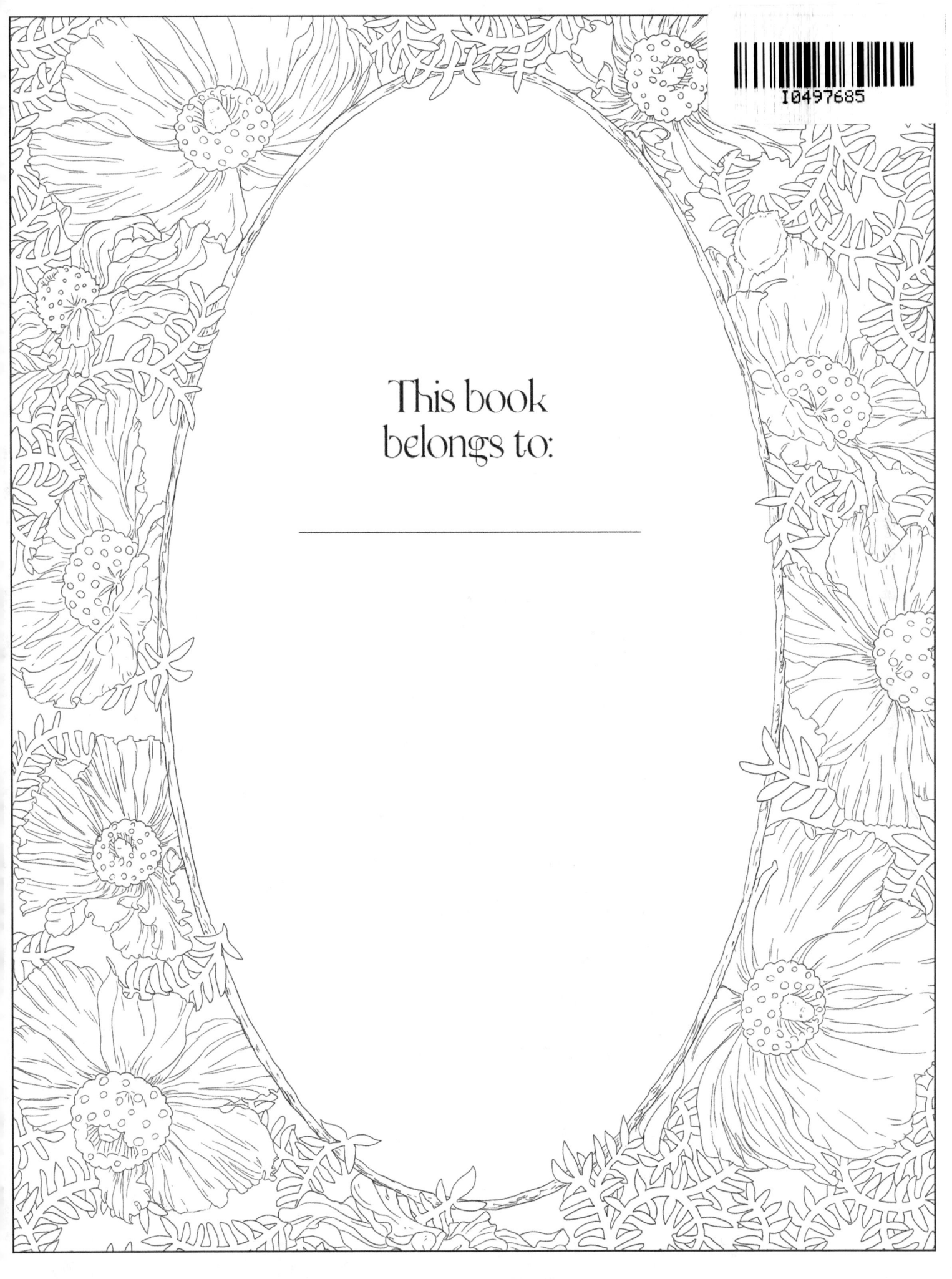

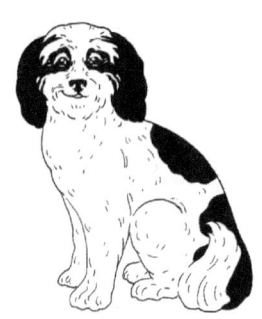

Copyright © 2021 by K.P. Singh

All rights reserved. No part of this book may be reproduced or used in any manner without written permission of the copyright owner except for the use of quotations in a book review. For more information, address: KPSingh.art@gmail.com

First paperback edition September 2021

KDP ISBN 9798482001738 (paperback)

www.KPSingh.art

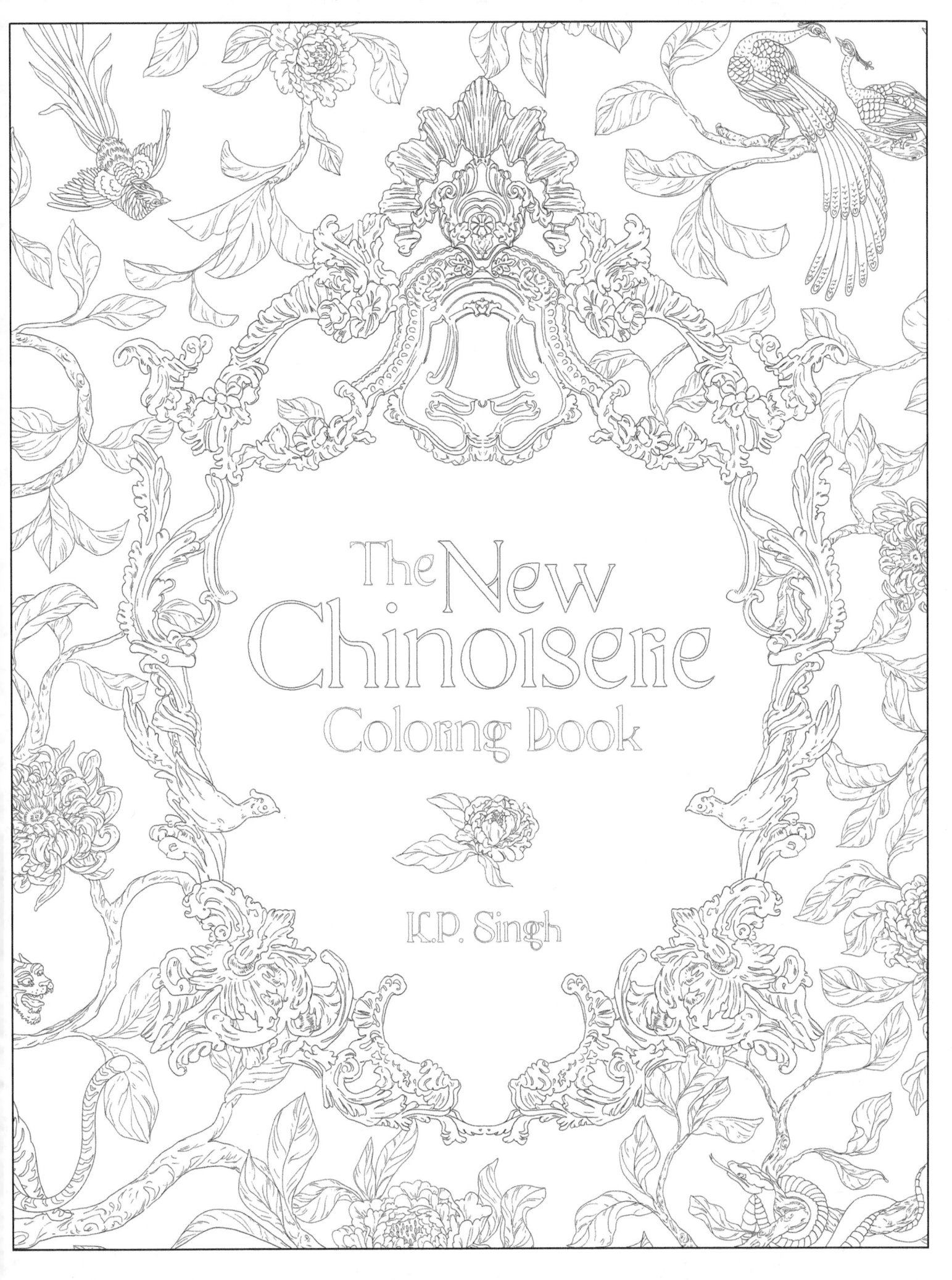

THANK YOU FOR COLORING

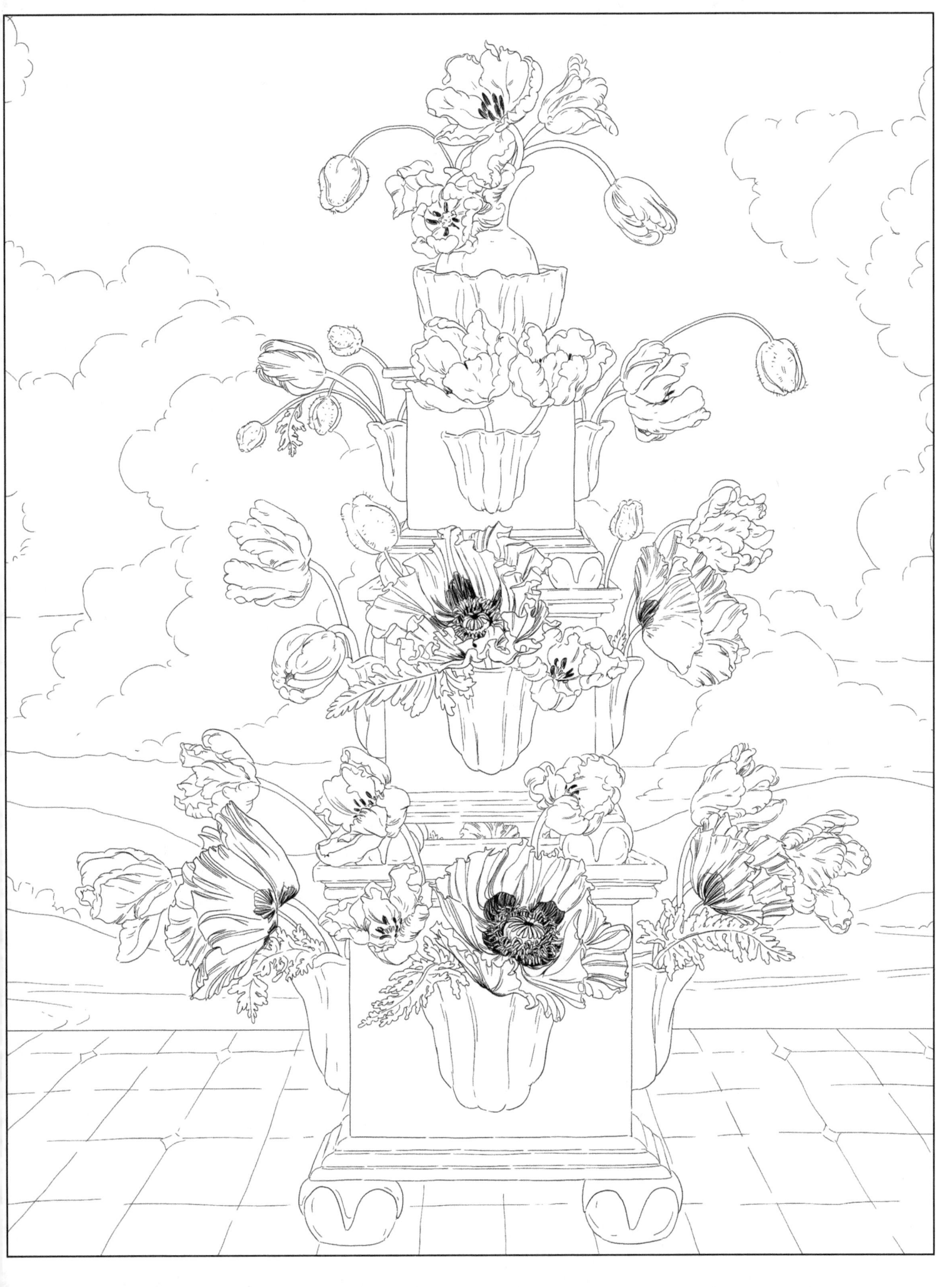

TULIPIERE WITH POPPIES

TULIPIERE WITH POPPIES

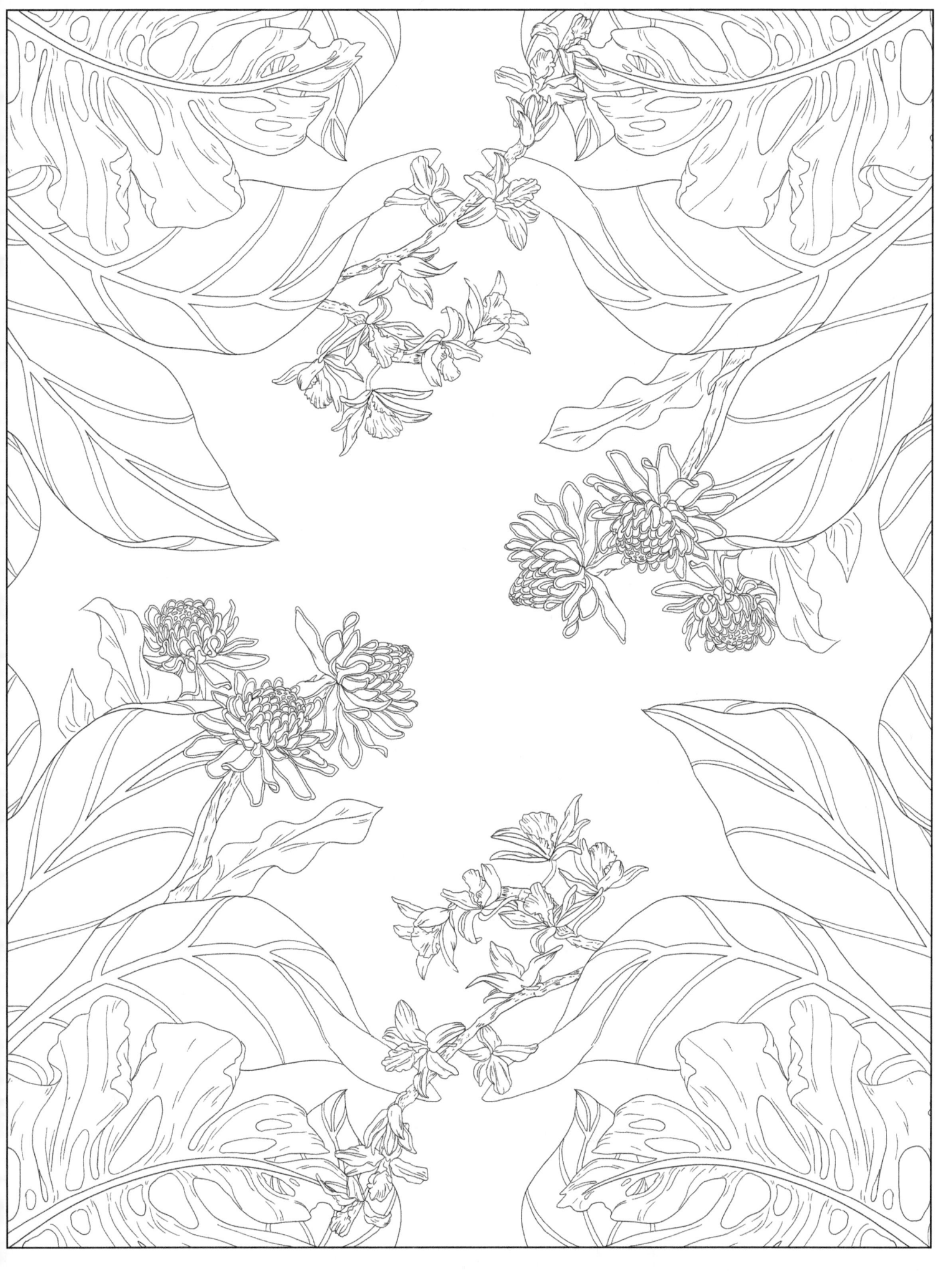

ORCHIDS AND GINGER

ORCHIDS AND GINGER

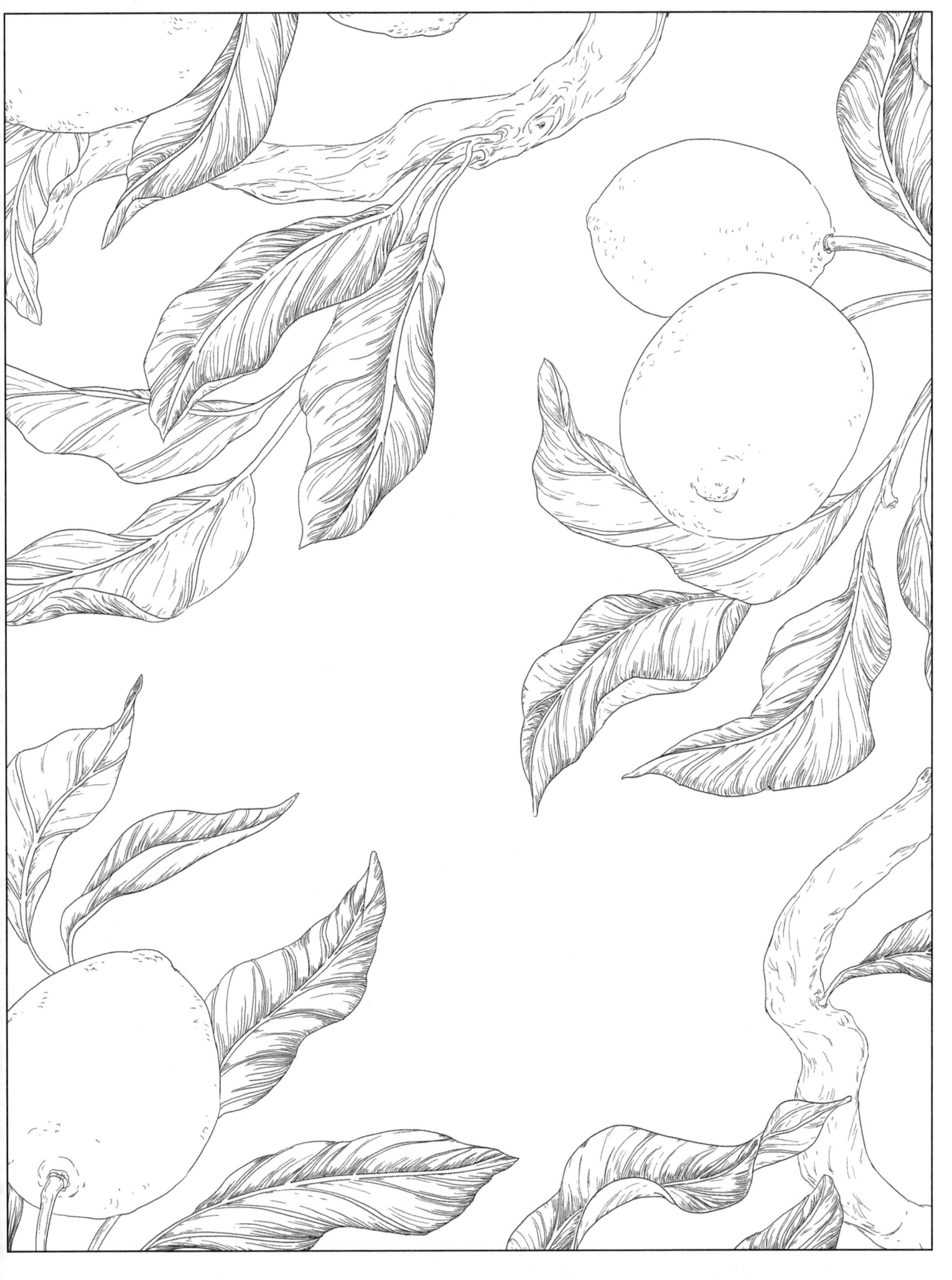

LEMON BRANCHES

LEMON BRANCHES

CERAMIC FRIEND

CERAMIC FRIEND

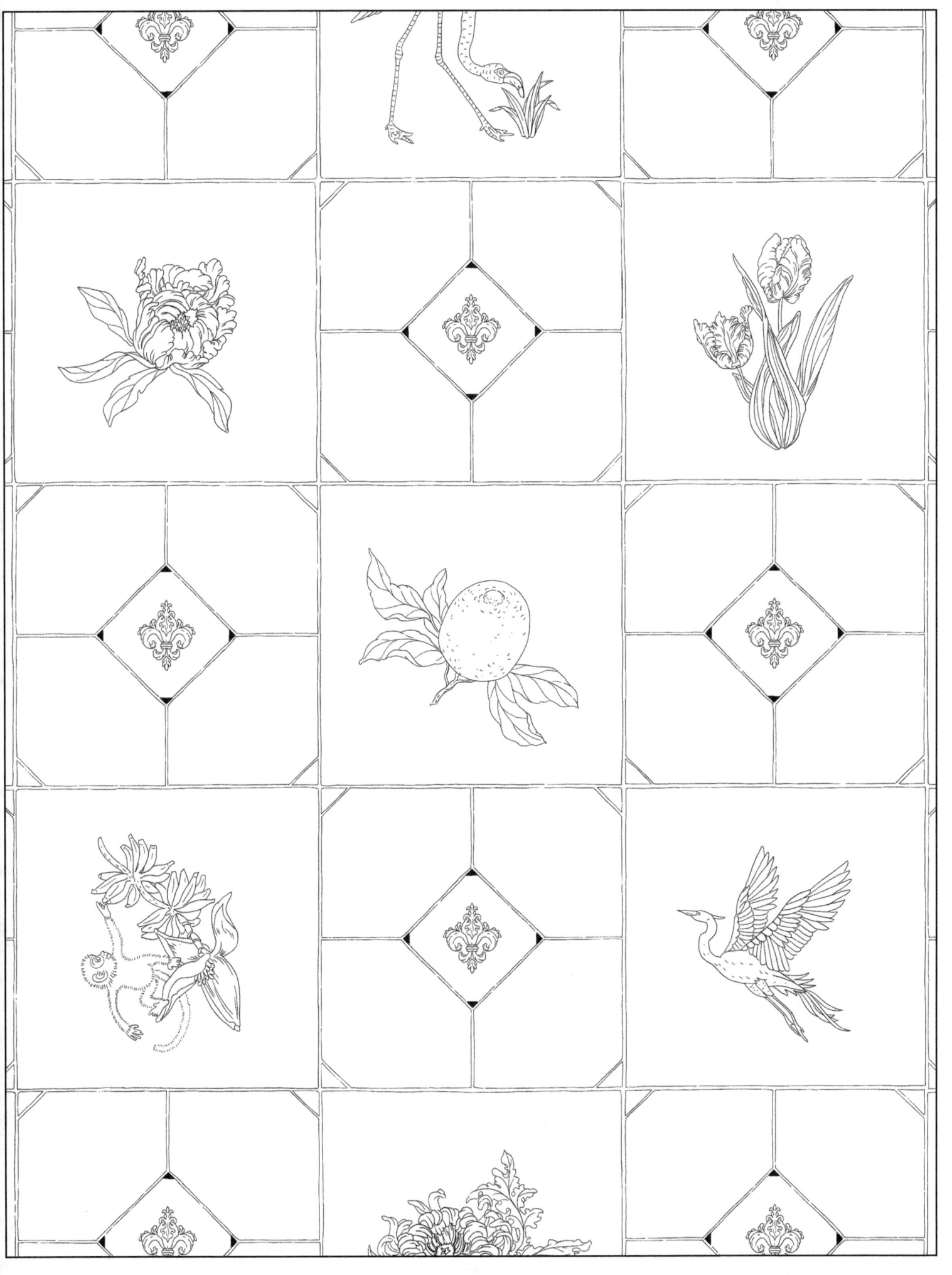

SQUARE TILES

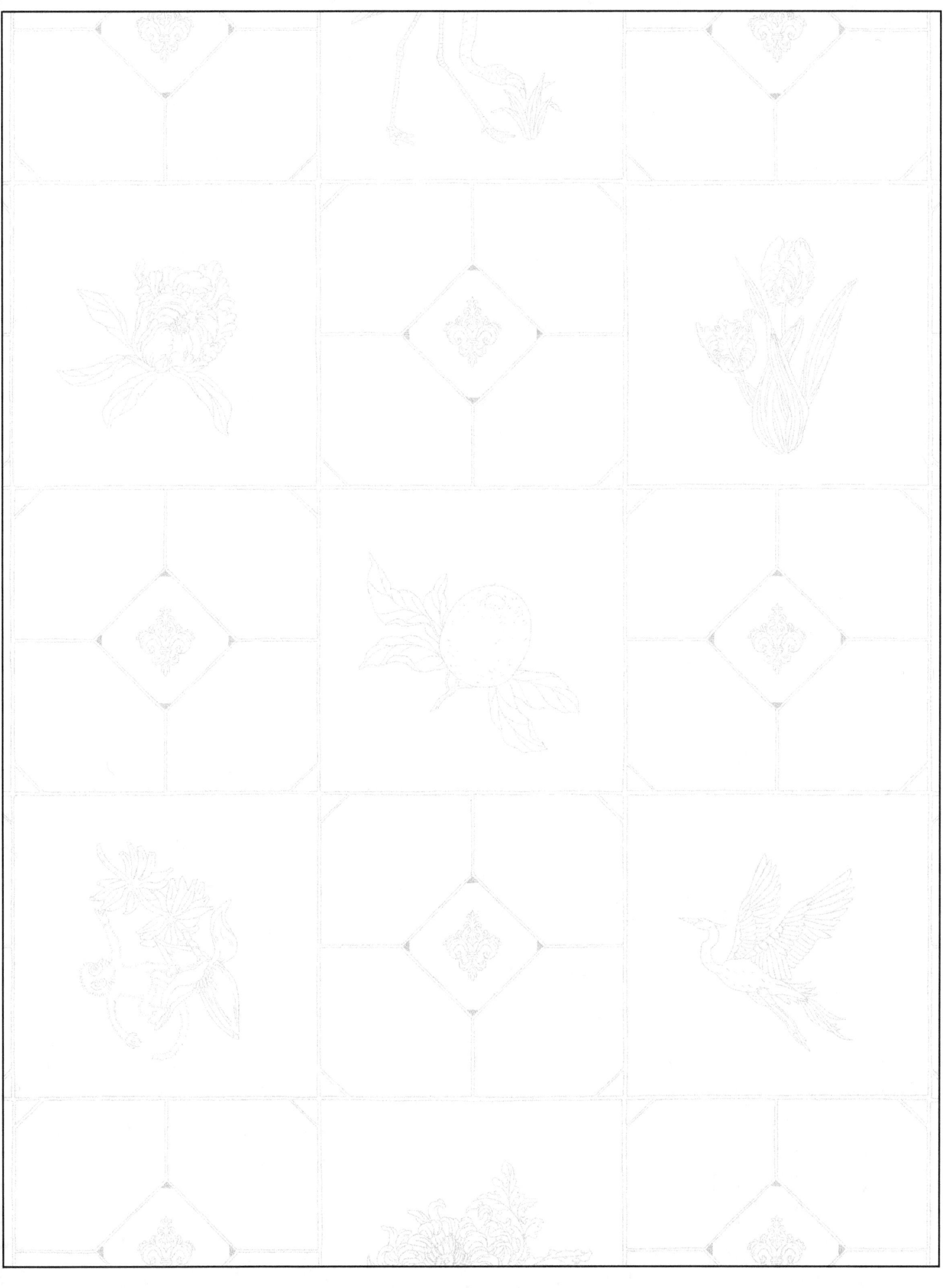

SQUARE TILES

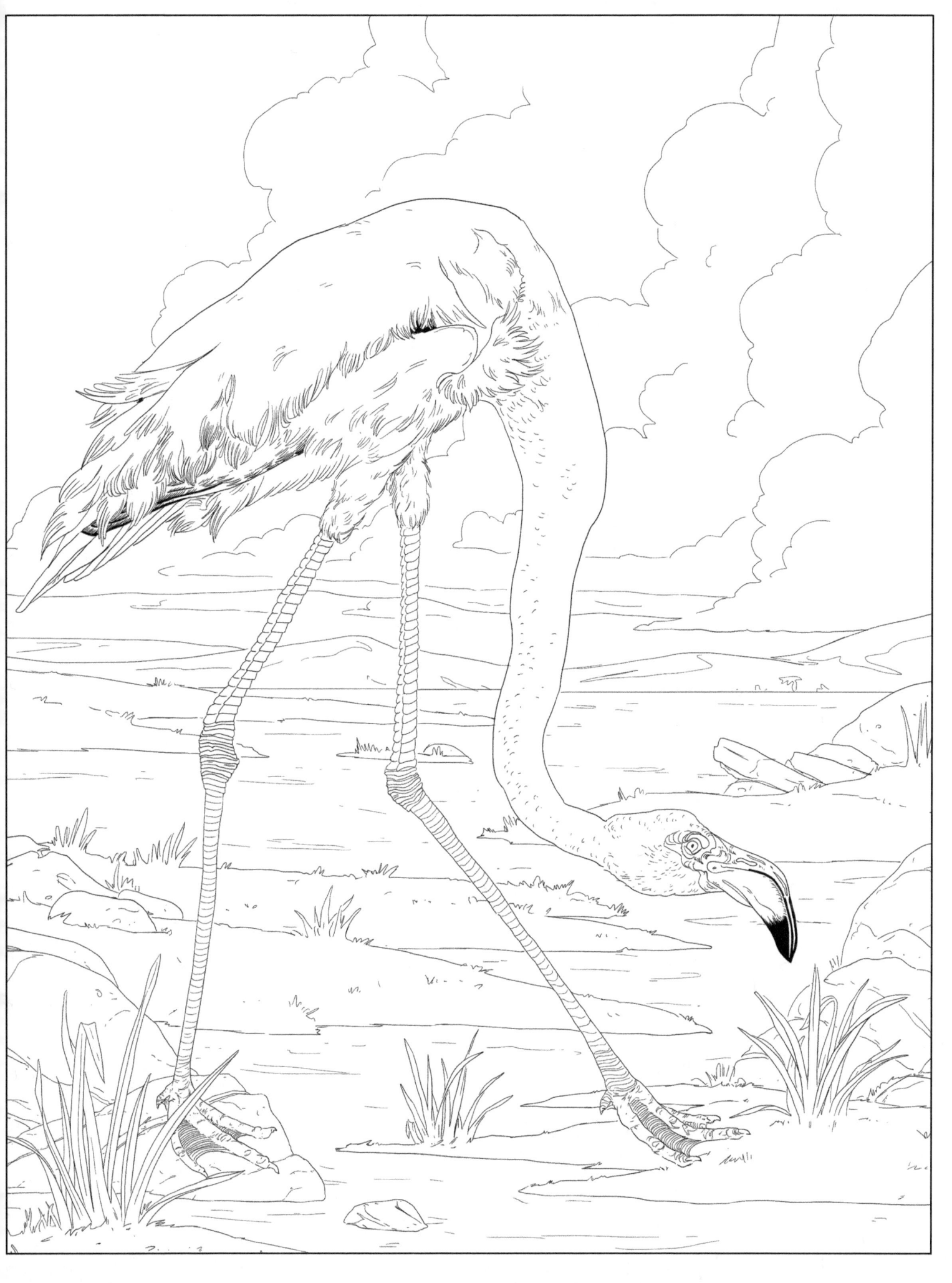

FLAMINGO SKULKING

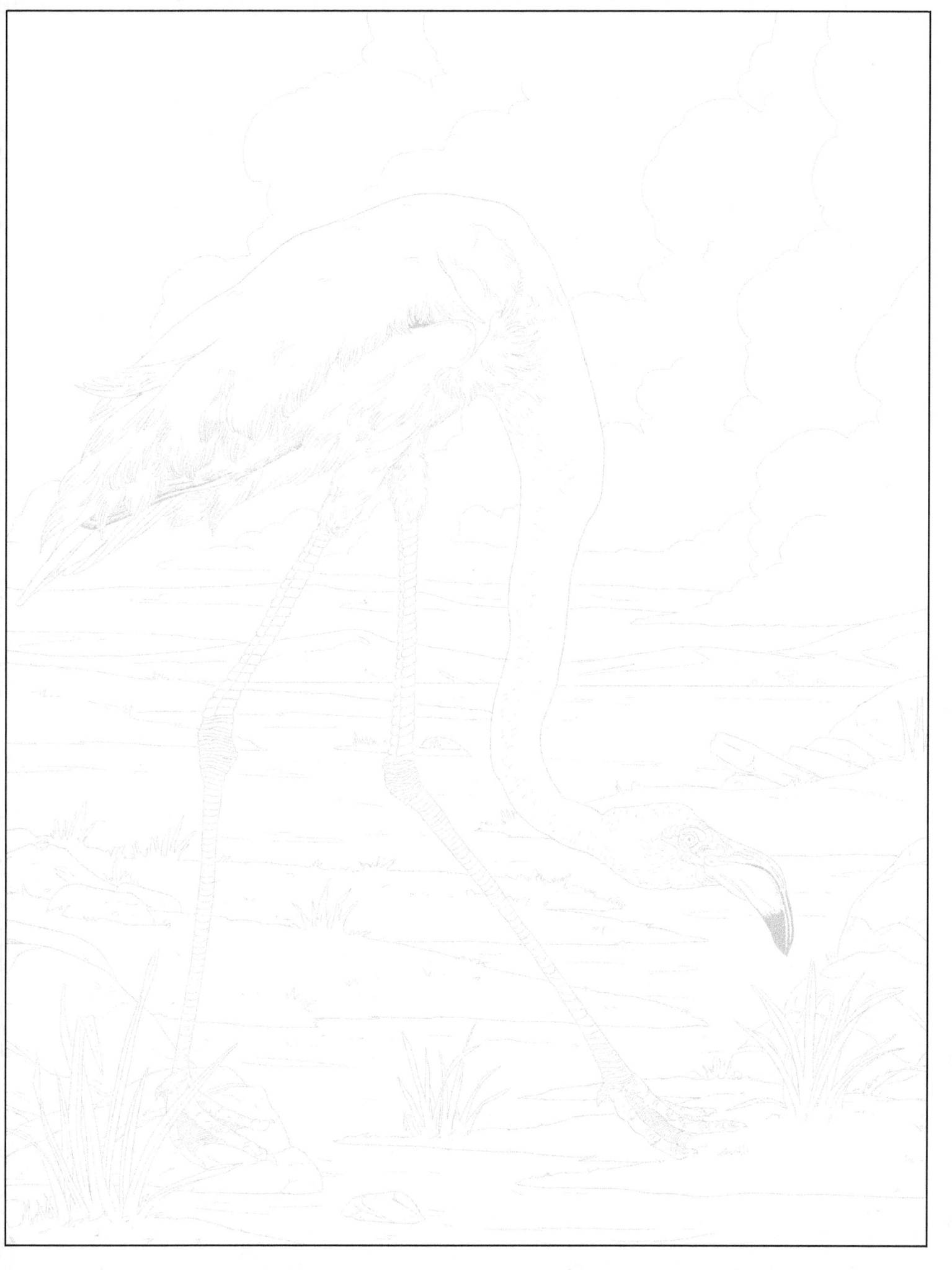

FLAMINGO SKULKING

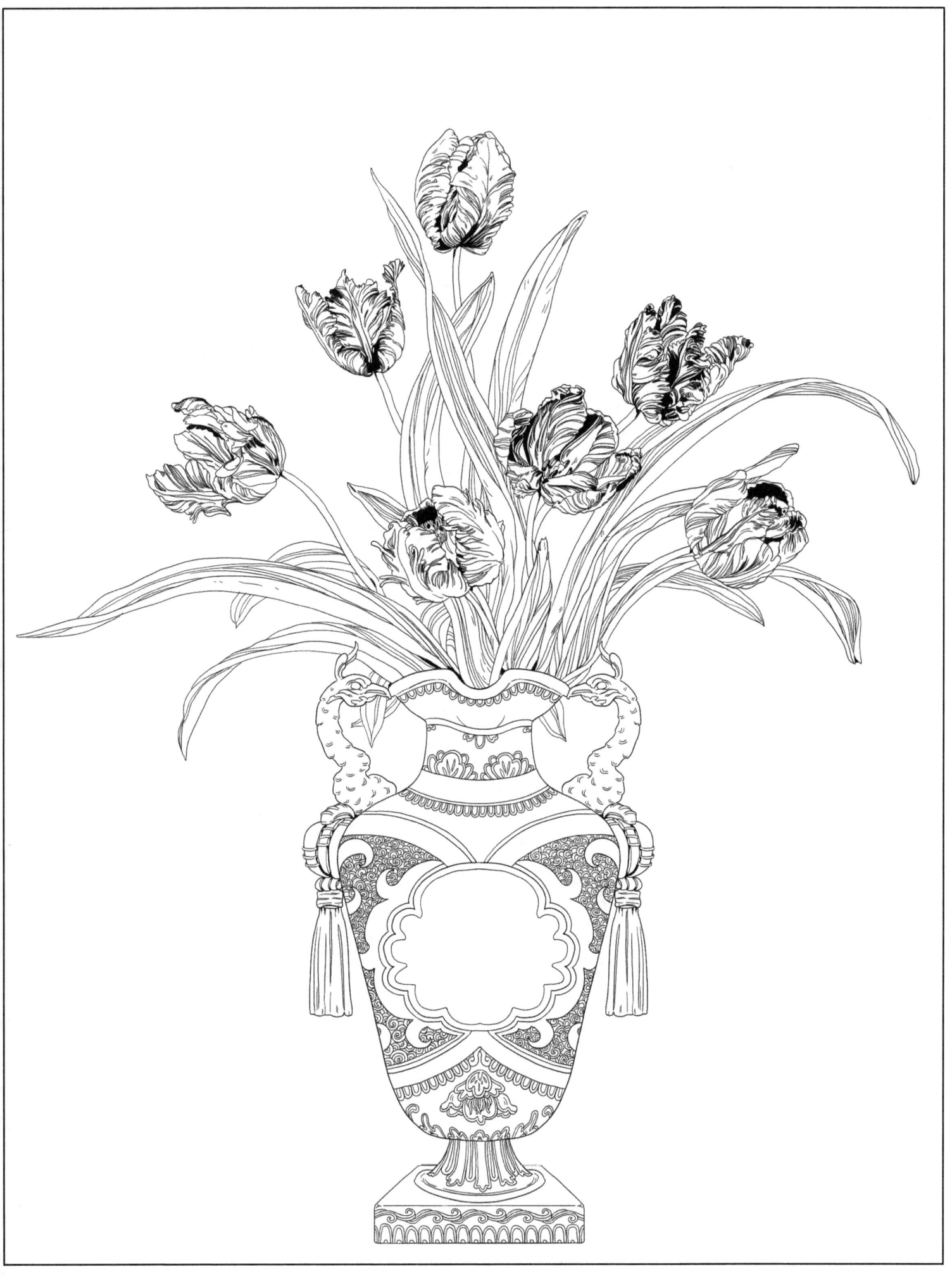

AN URN WITH TULIPS

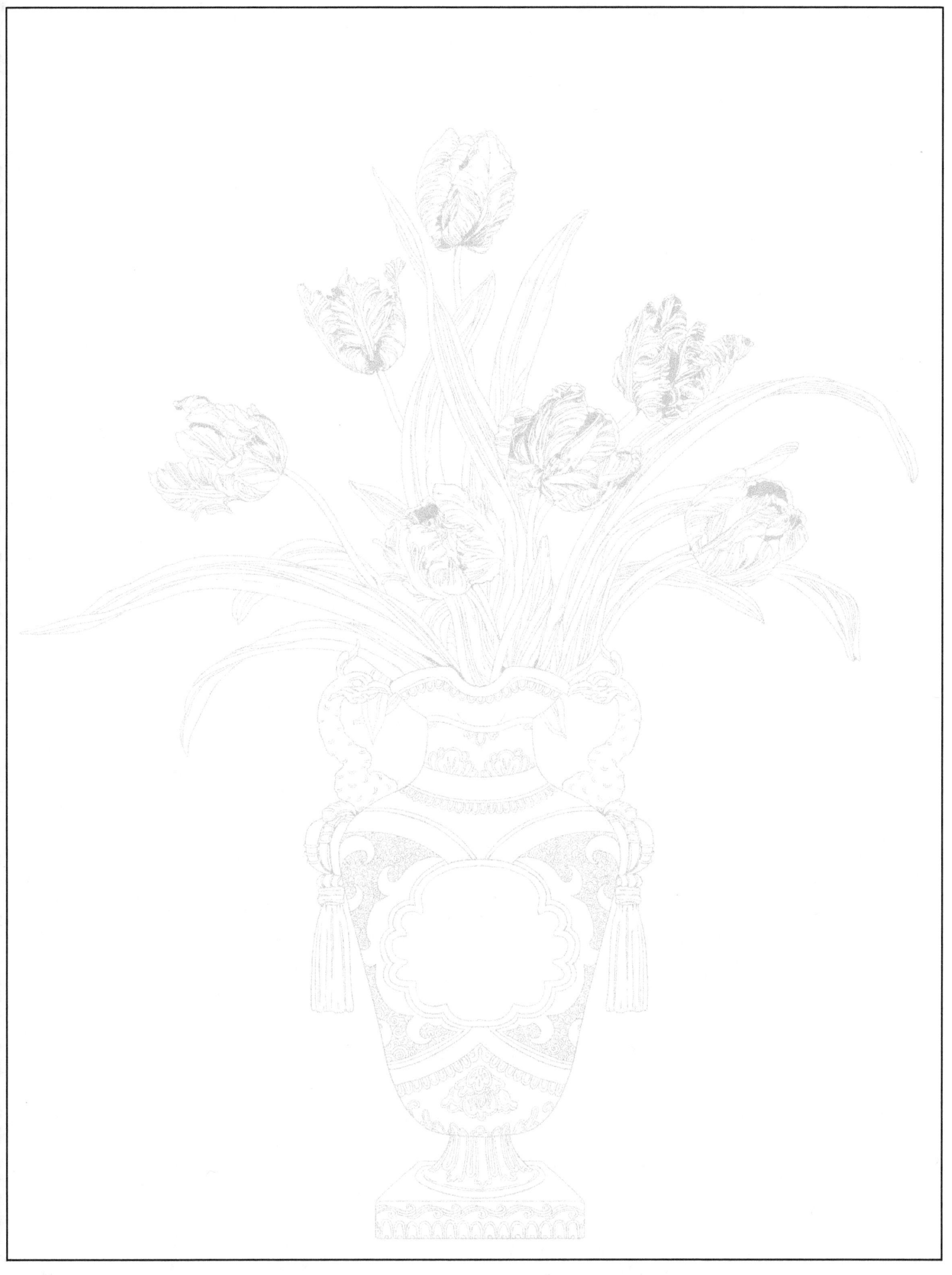

AN URN WITH TULIPS

CHRYSANTHEMUM STEMS

CHRYSANTHEMUM STEMS

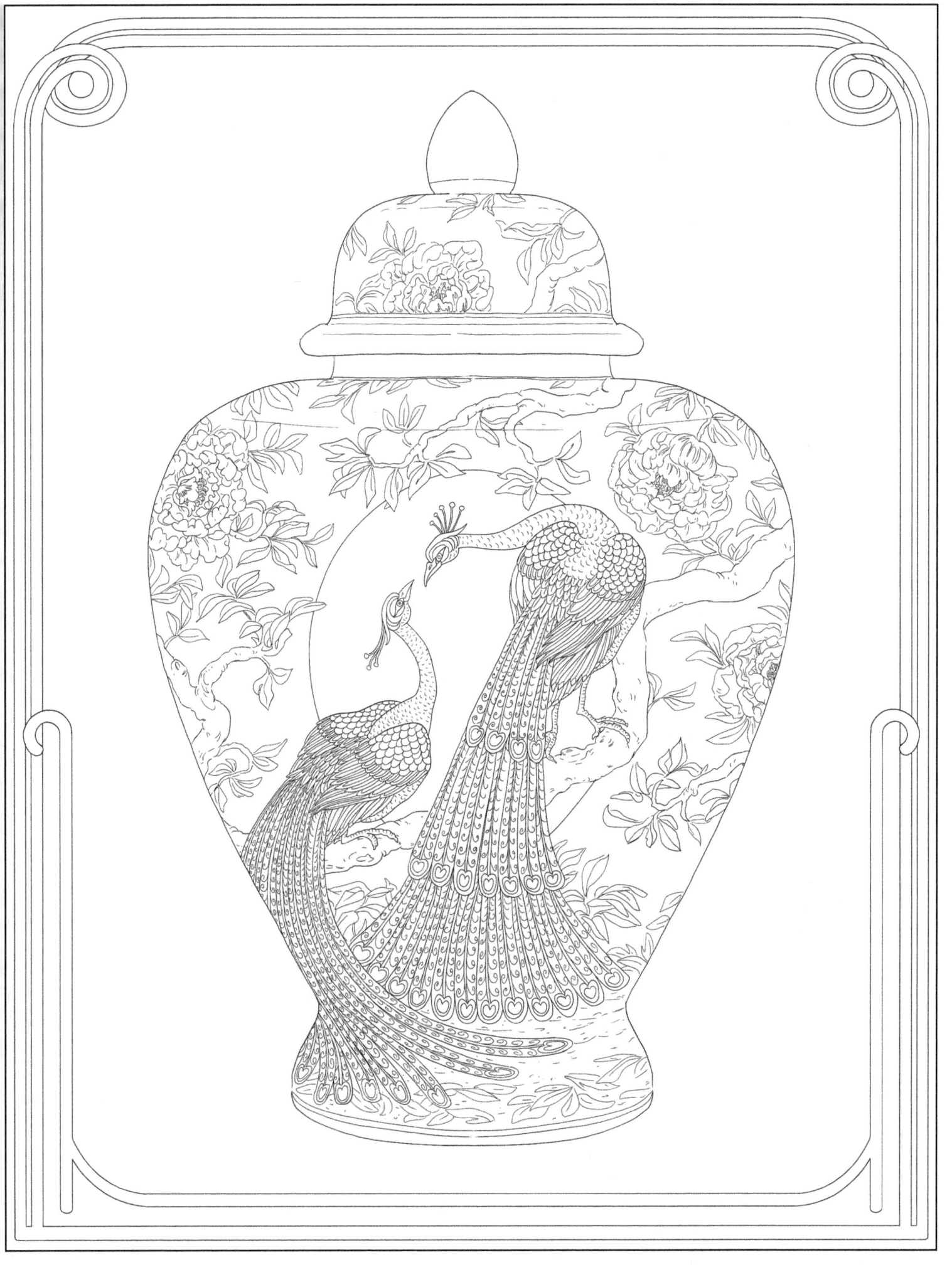

PEACOCK GINGER JAR

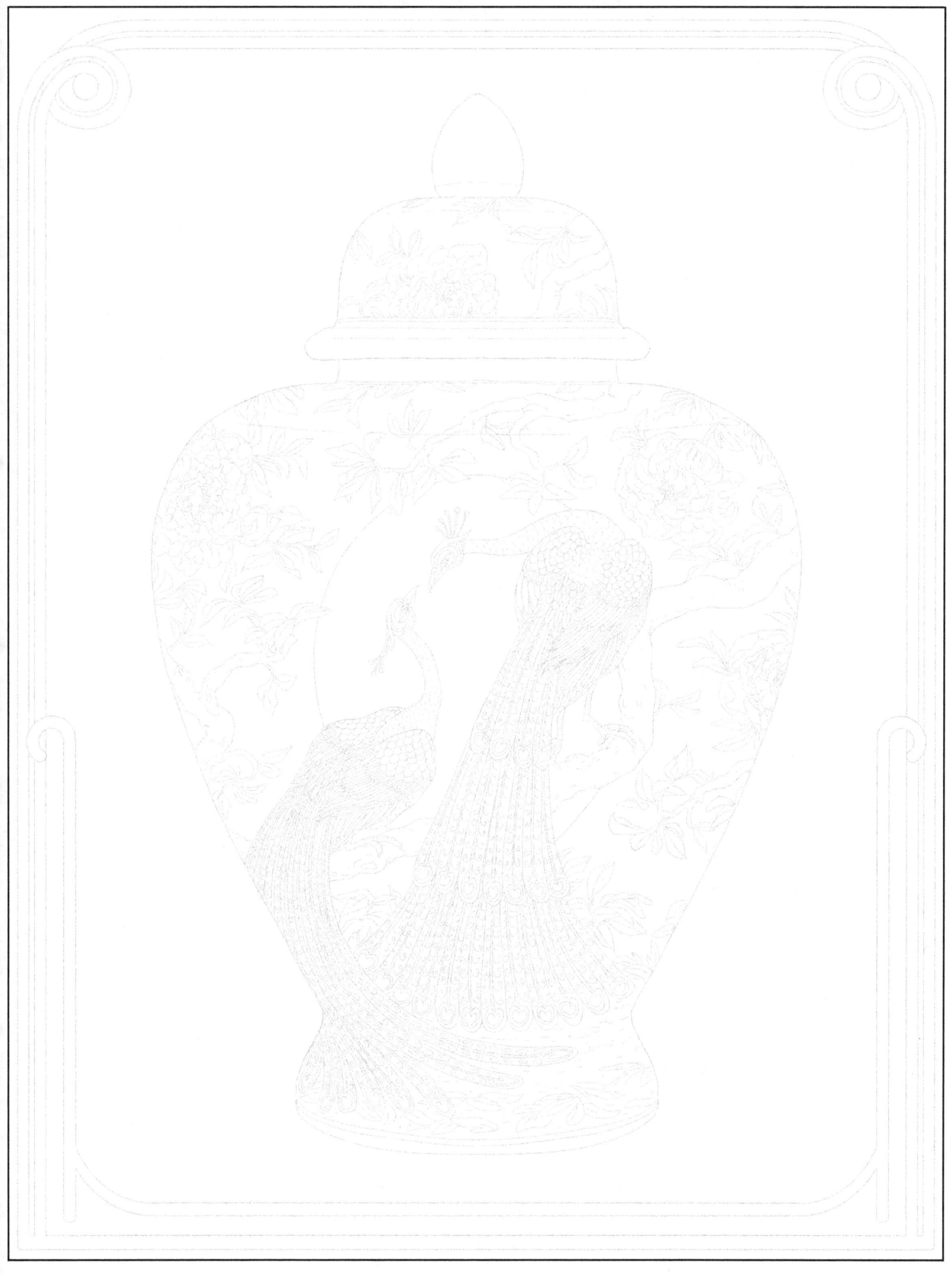

PEACOCK GINGER JAR

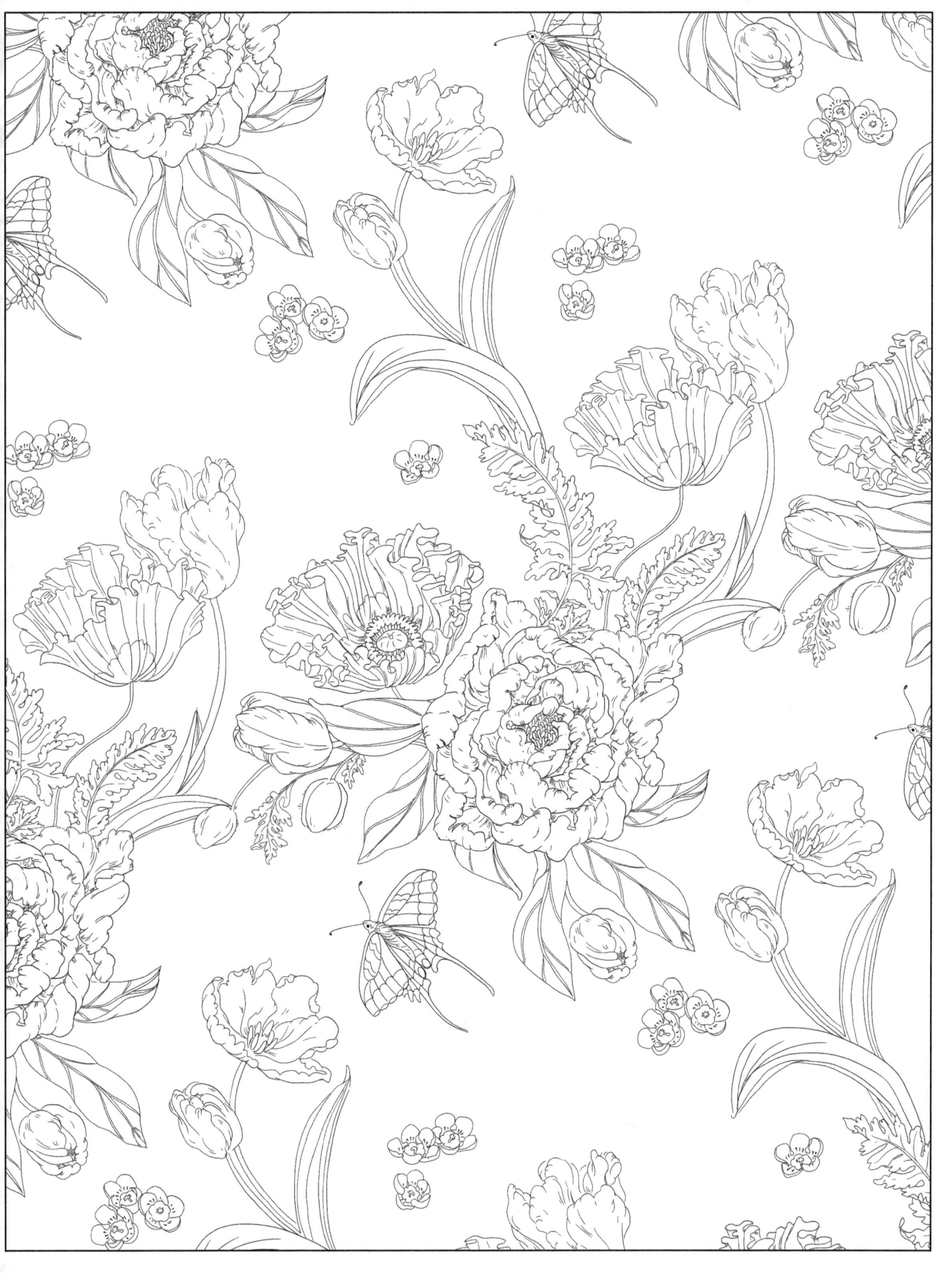

BOTANICAL WALLPAPER

BOTANICAL WALLPAPER

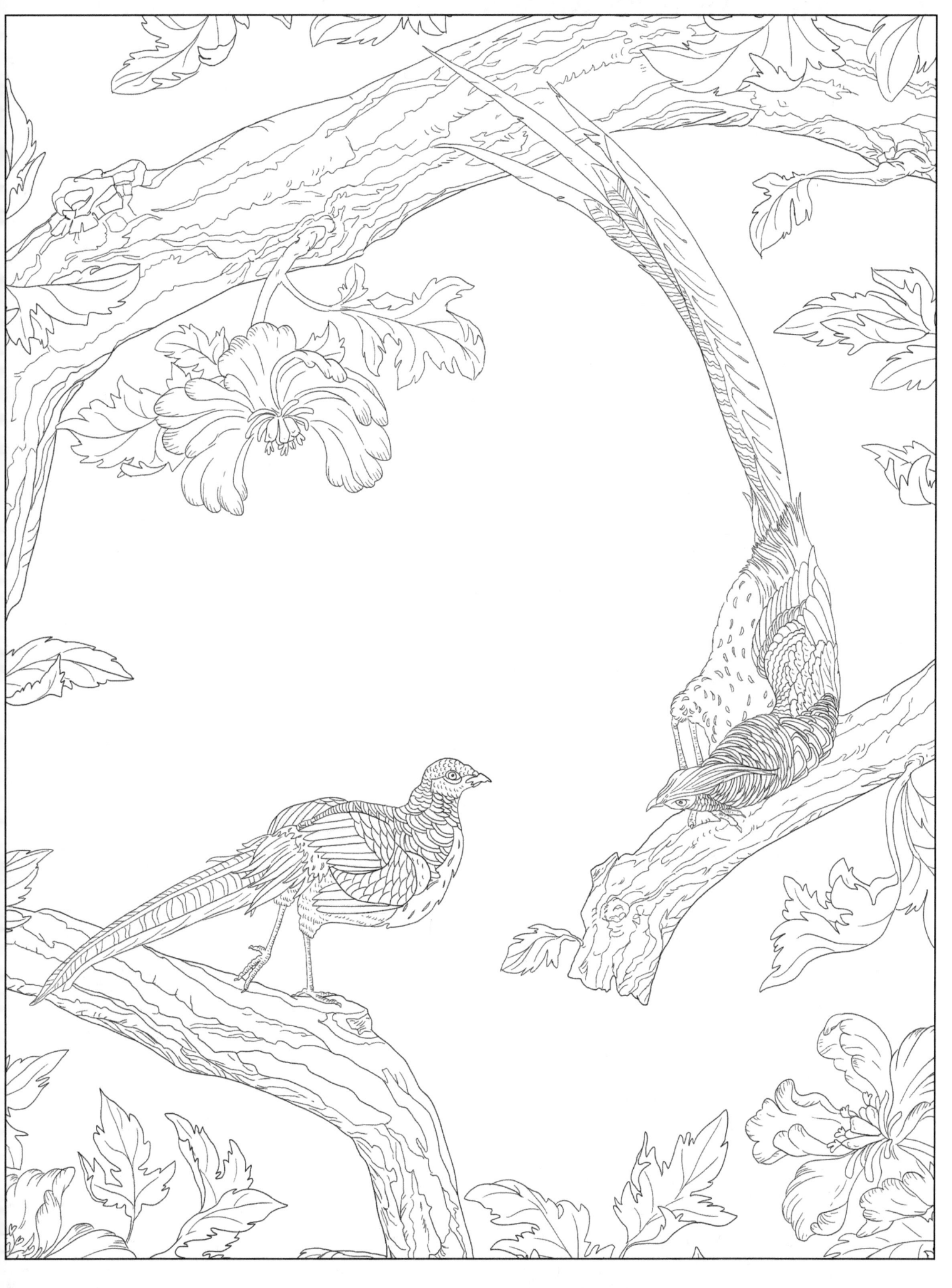

PHEASANTS COURTING

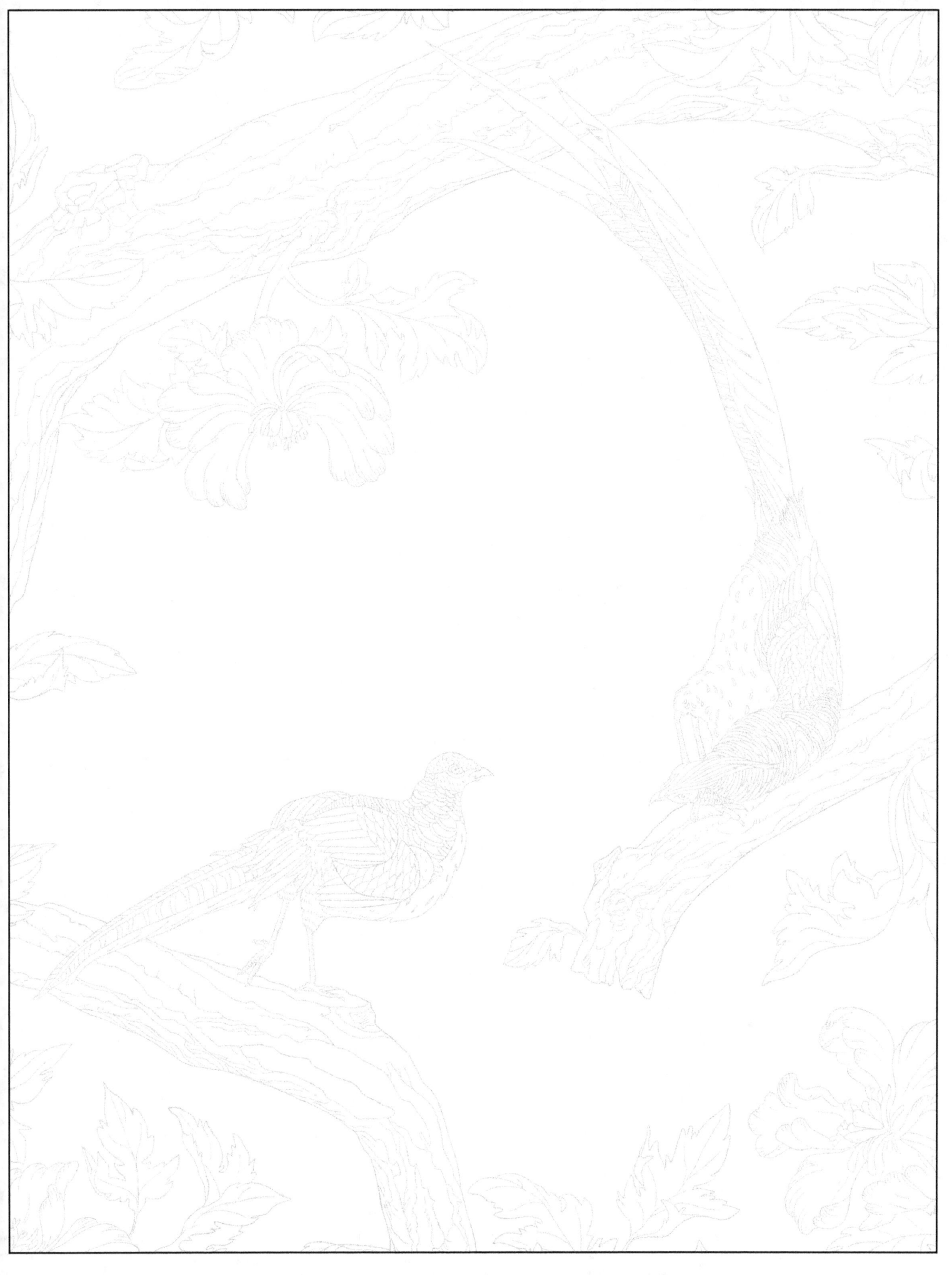

PHEASANTS COURTING

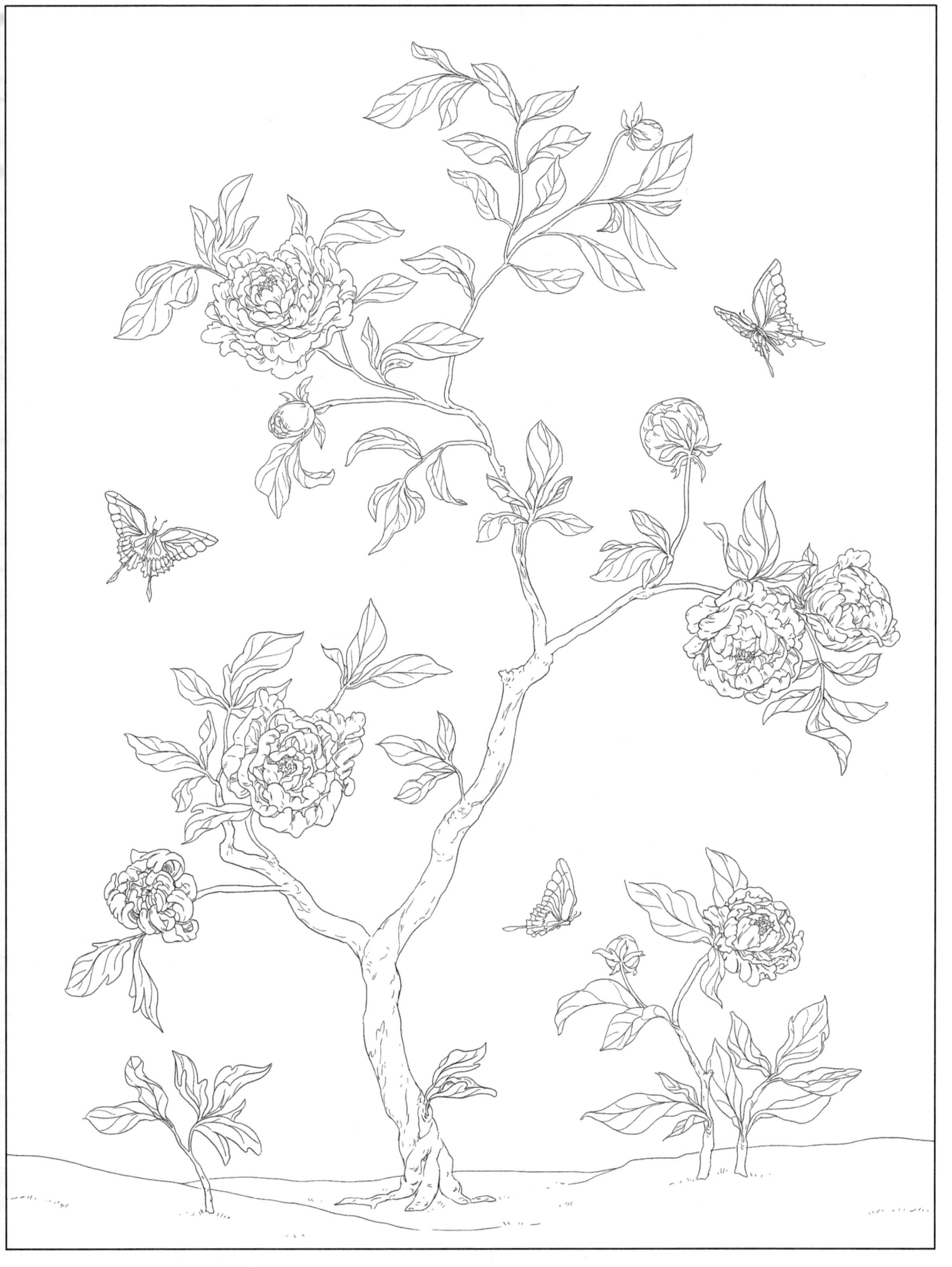

CLASSIC TREE PEONY

CLASSIC TREE PEONY

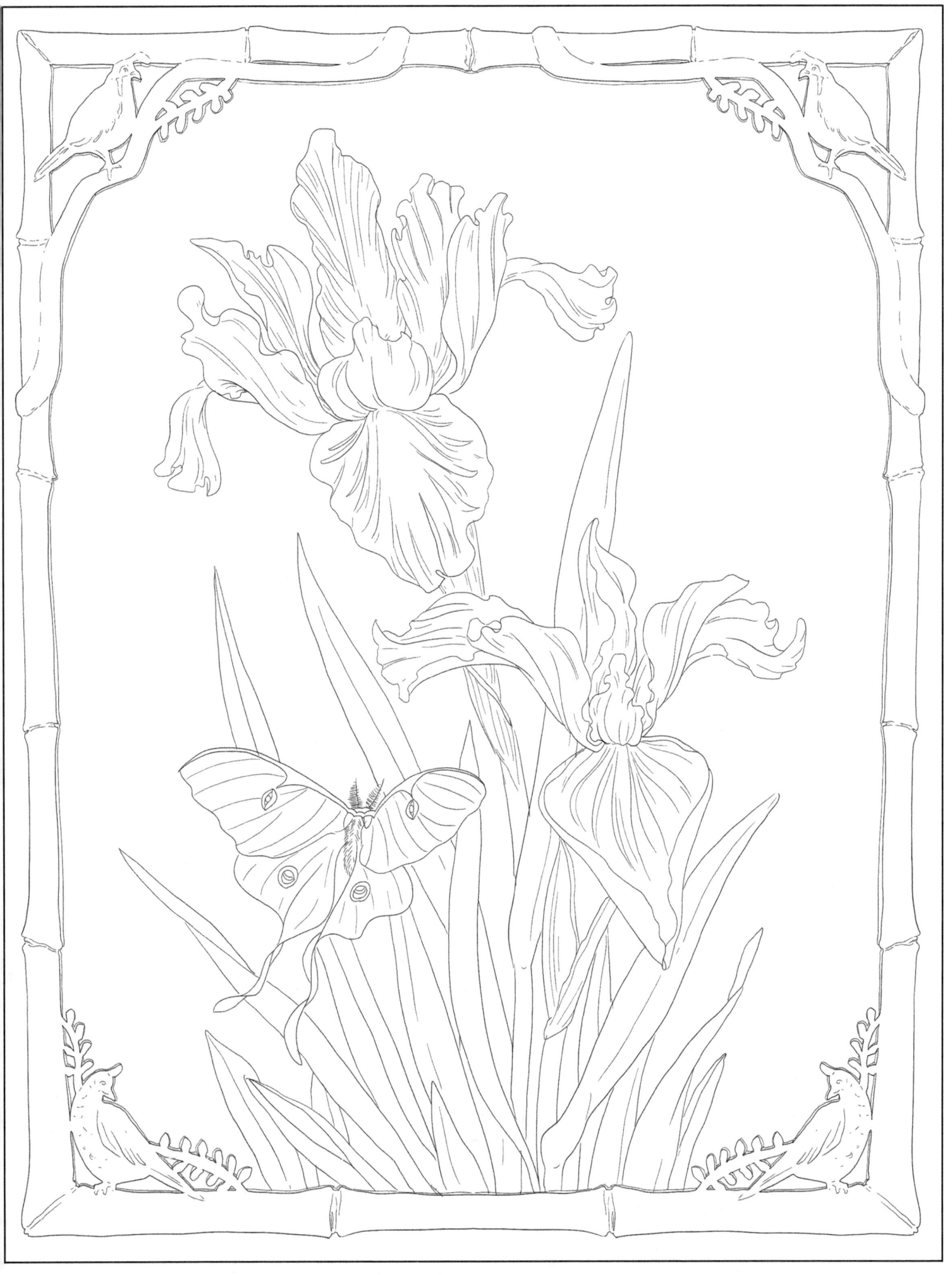

IRISES IN A WOOD FRAME

IRISES IN A WOOD FRAME

PEONY AND TIGER MOTIF

PEONY AND TIGER MOTIF

SEVEN PETALED FLOWER PATTERN

SEVEN PETALED FLOWER PATTERN

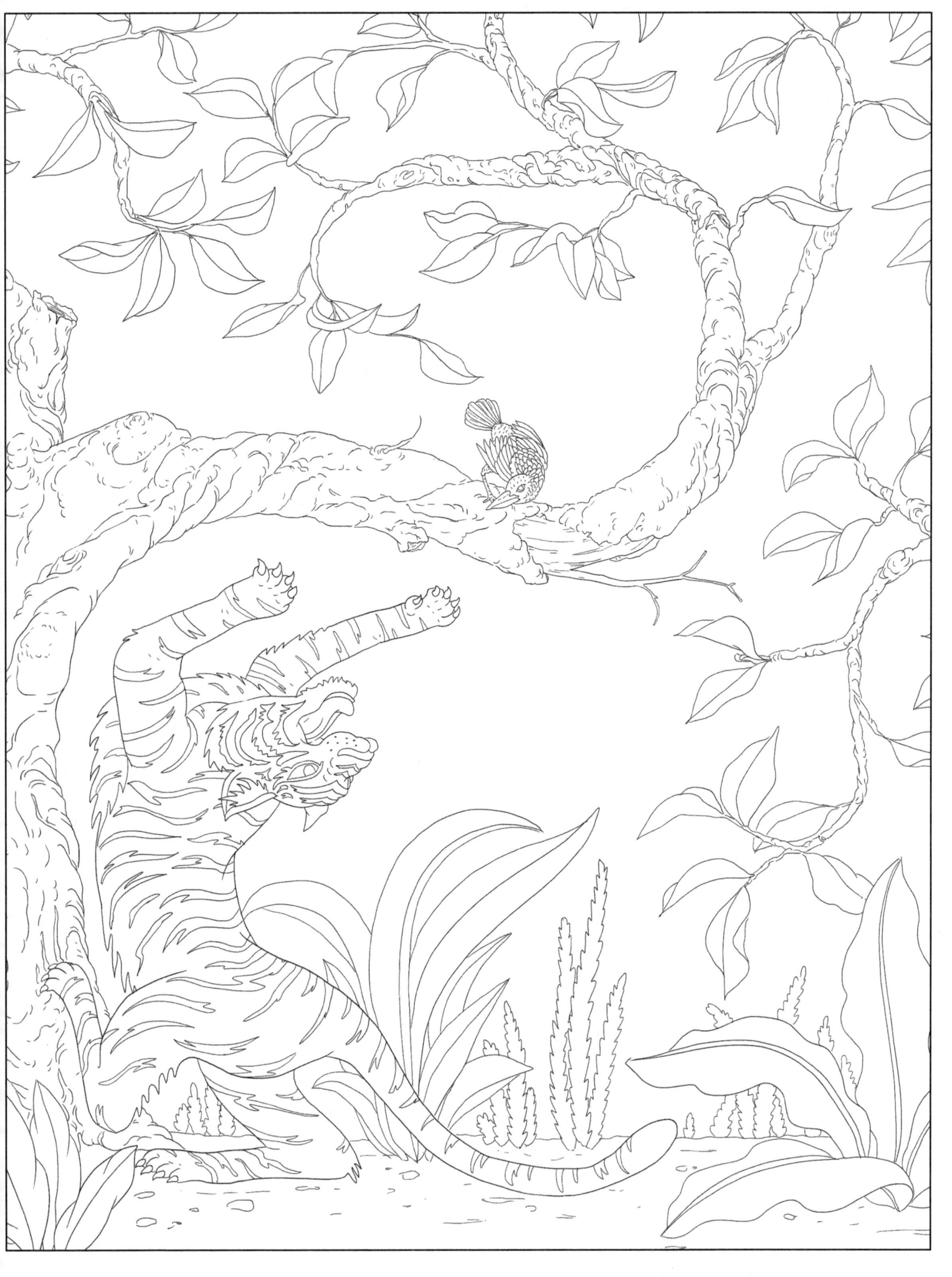

KINGFISHER TEASING THE TIGER

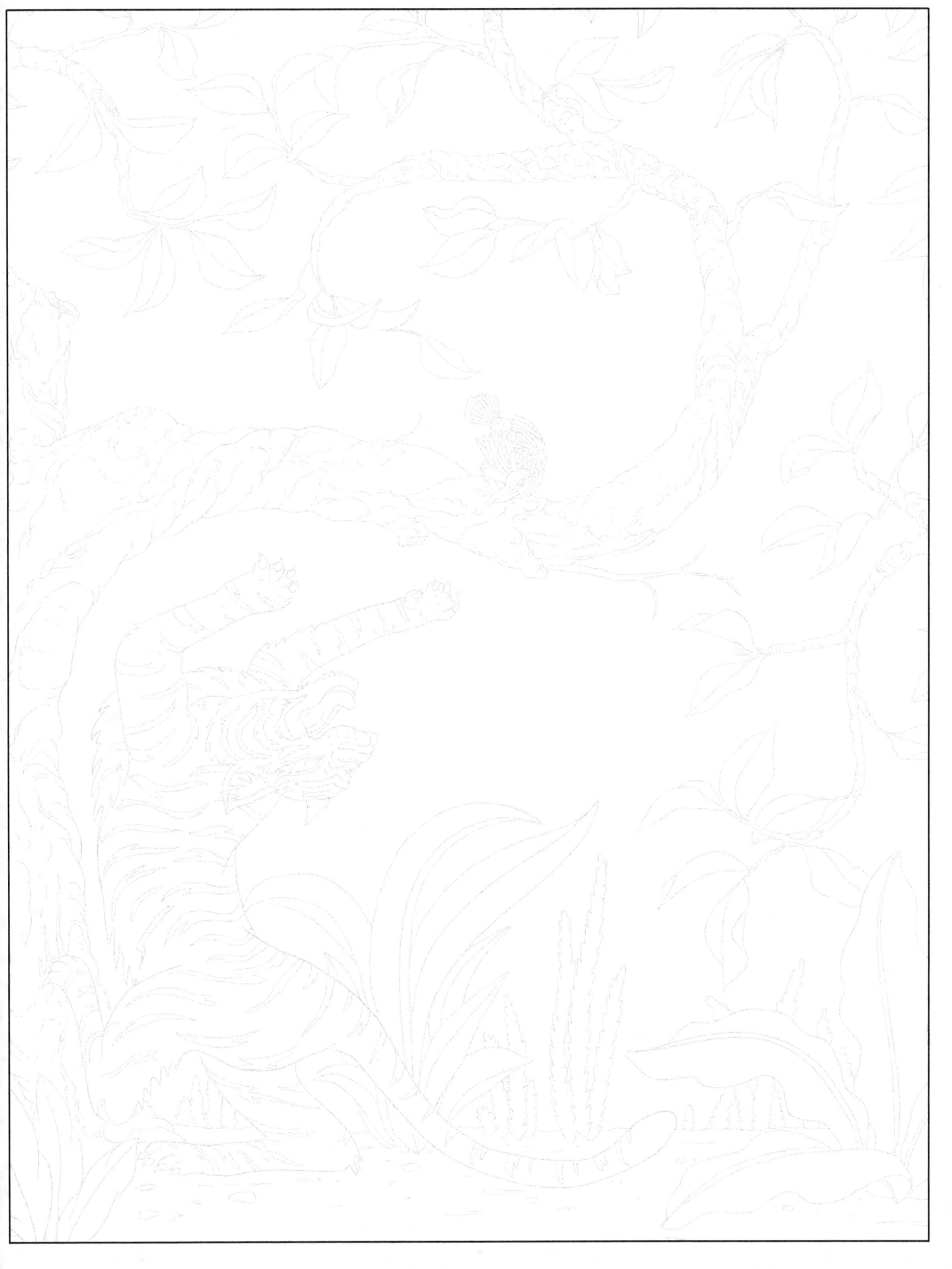

KINGFISHER TEASING THE TIGER

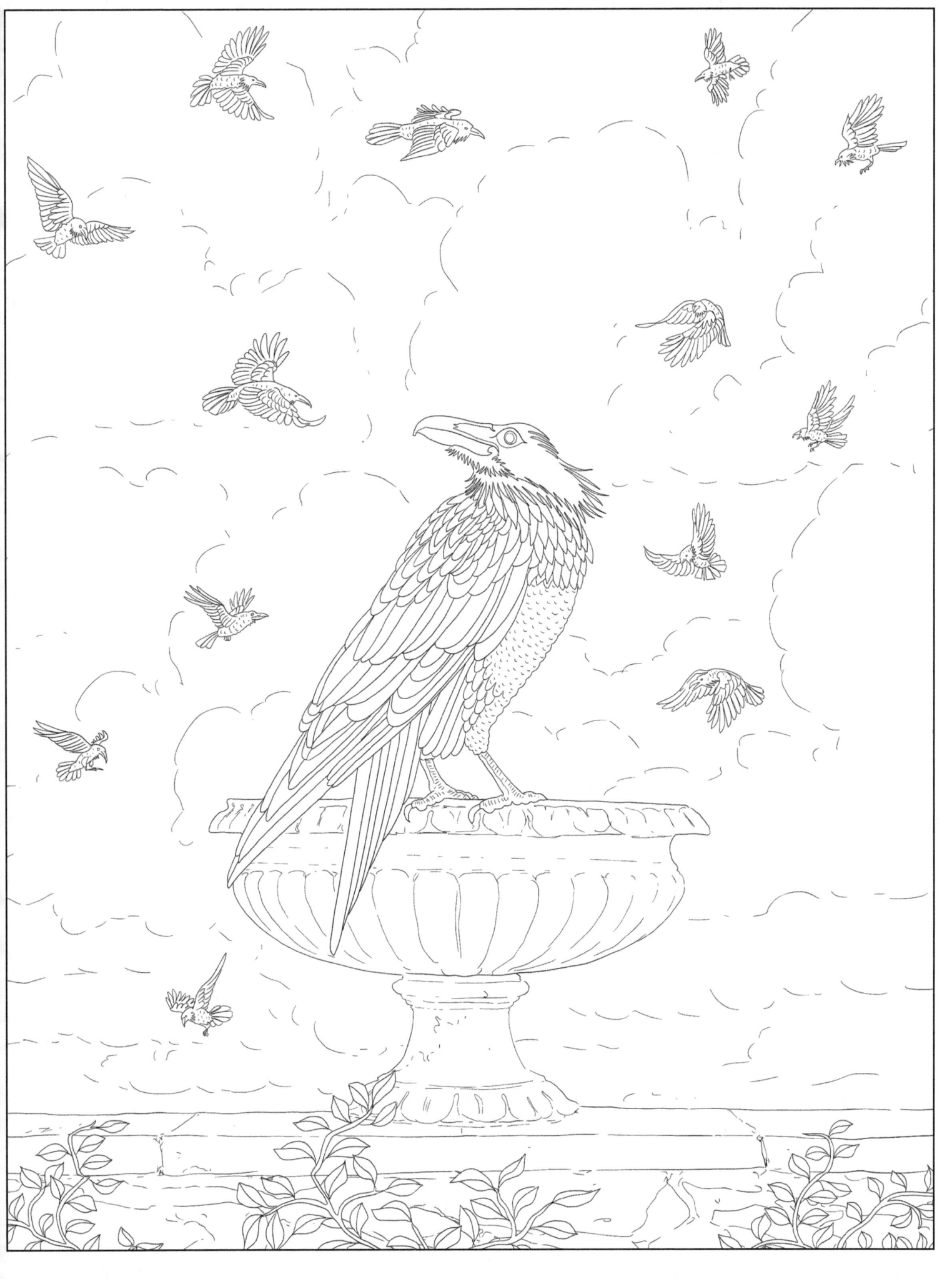

MY THANKS TO GOREY

MY THANKS TO GOREY

SINGLE PEONY MOTIF

SINGLE PEONY MOTIF

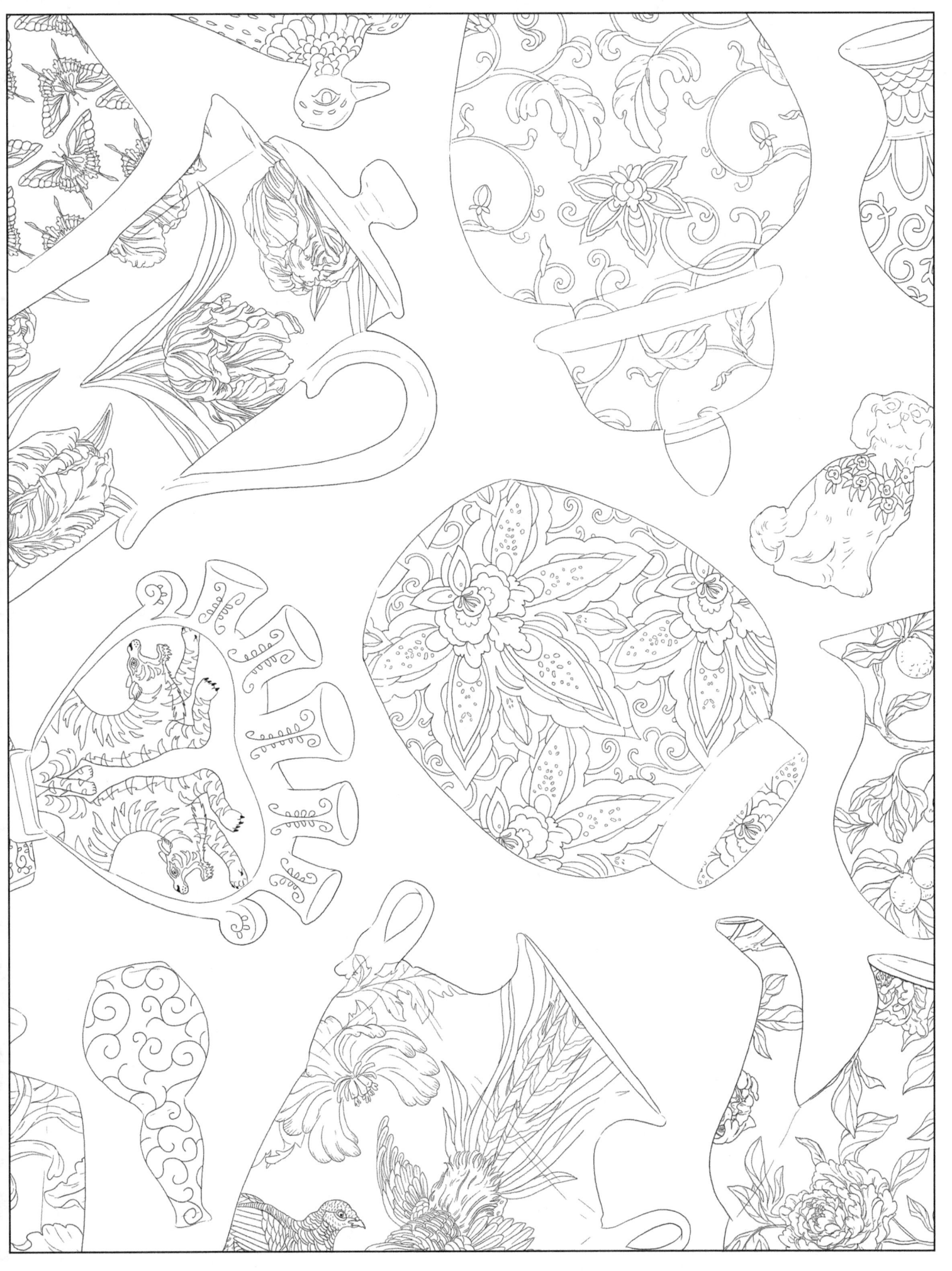

SCATTERED CERAMICS

SCATTERED CERAMICS

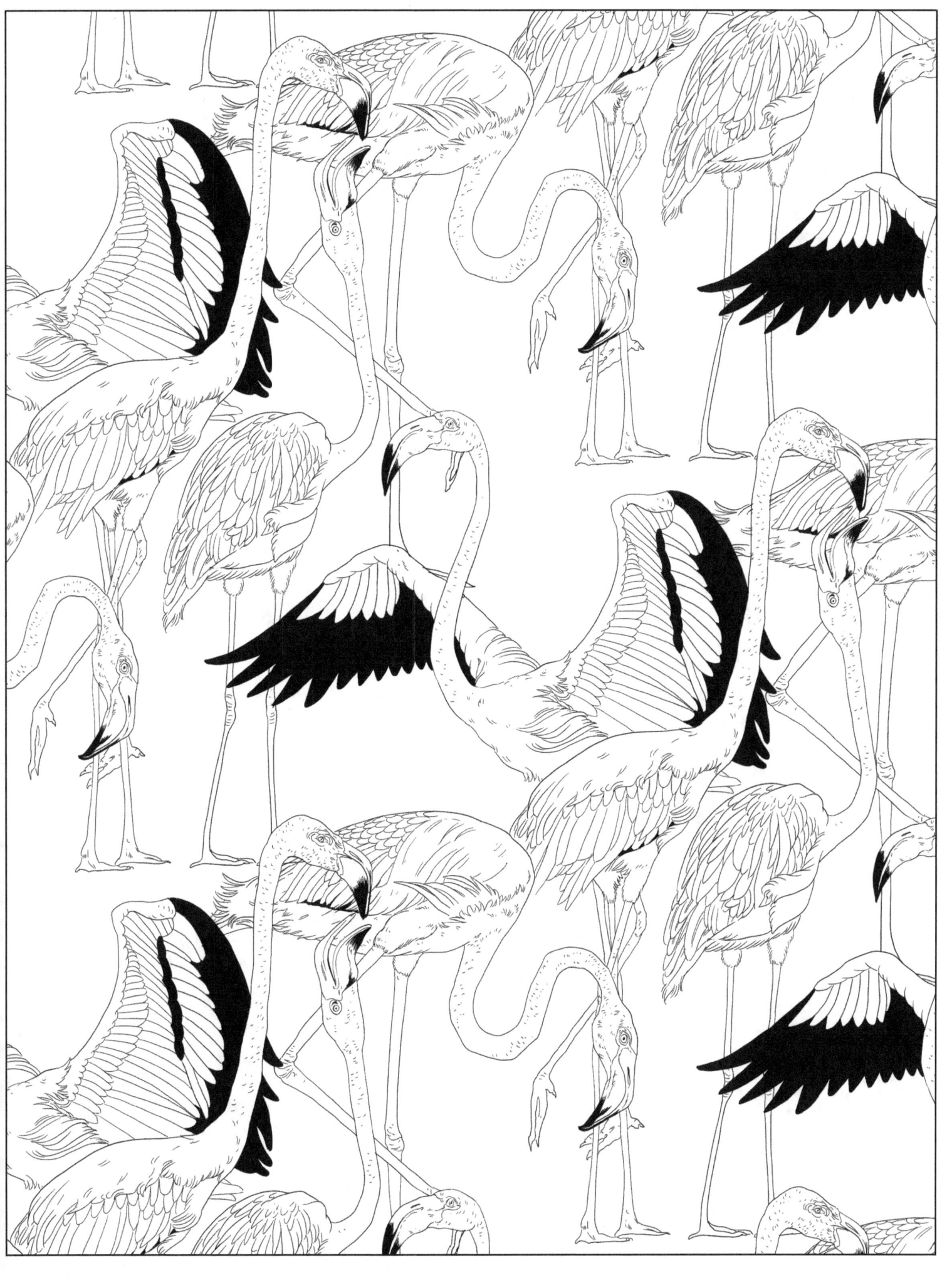

ENDLESS FLAMINGOES

ENDLESS FLAMINGOES

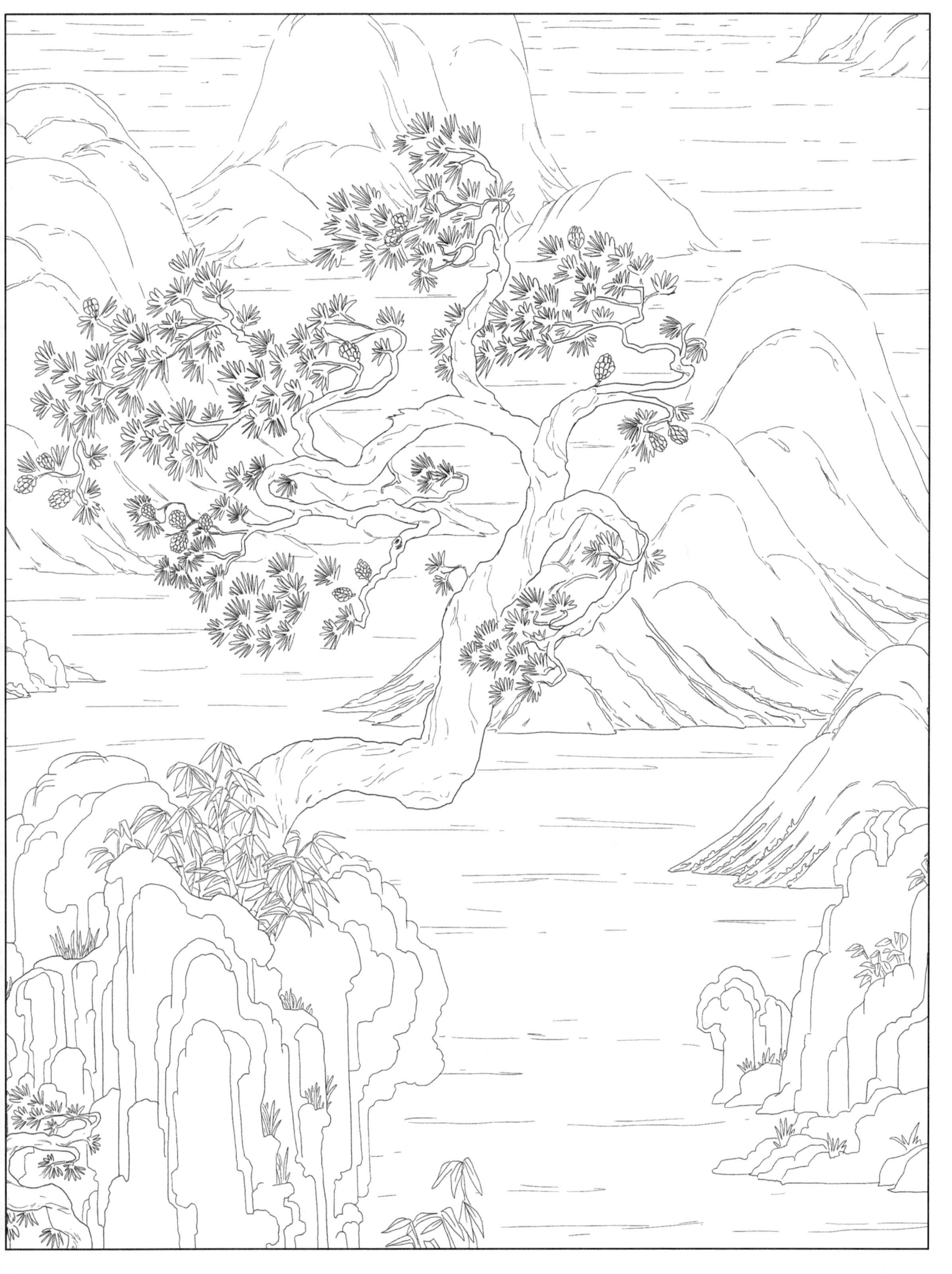

PINE TREE V. WIND

PINE TREE V. WIND

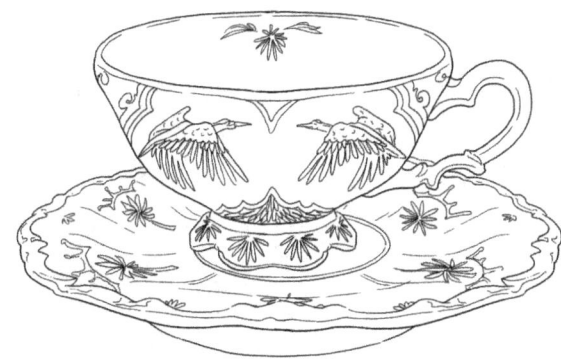
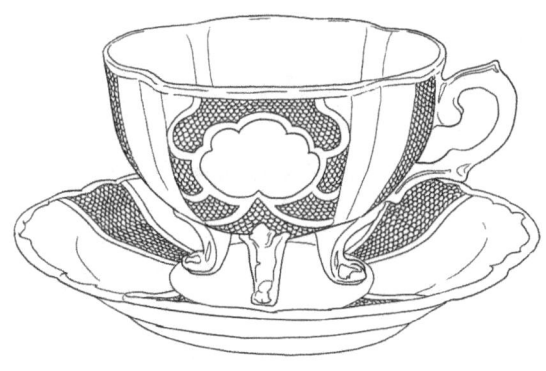
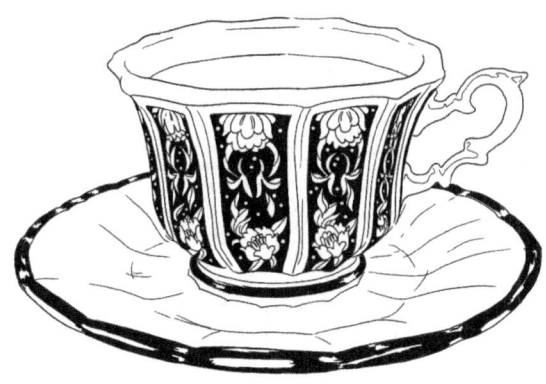
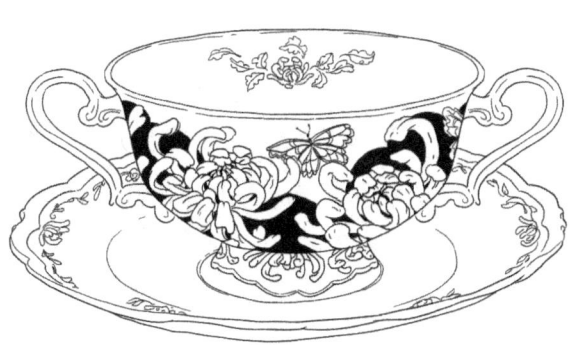
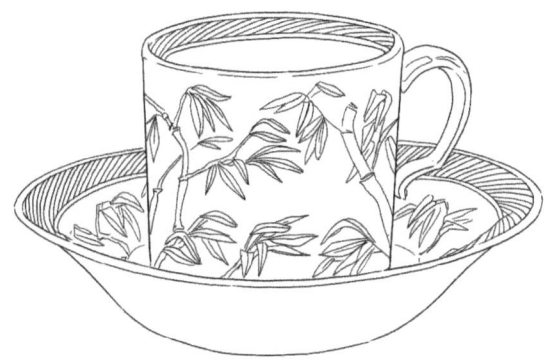
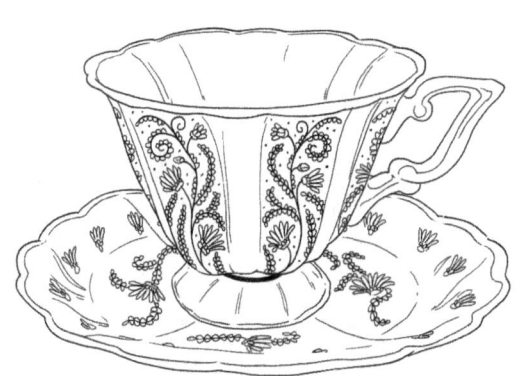

TEACUP SAMPLE

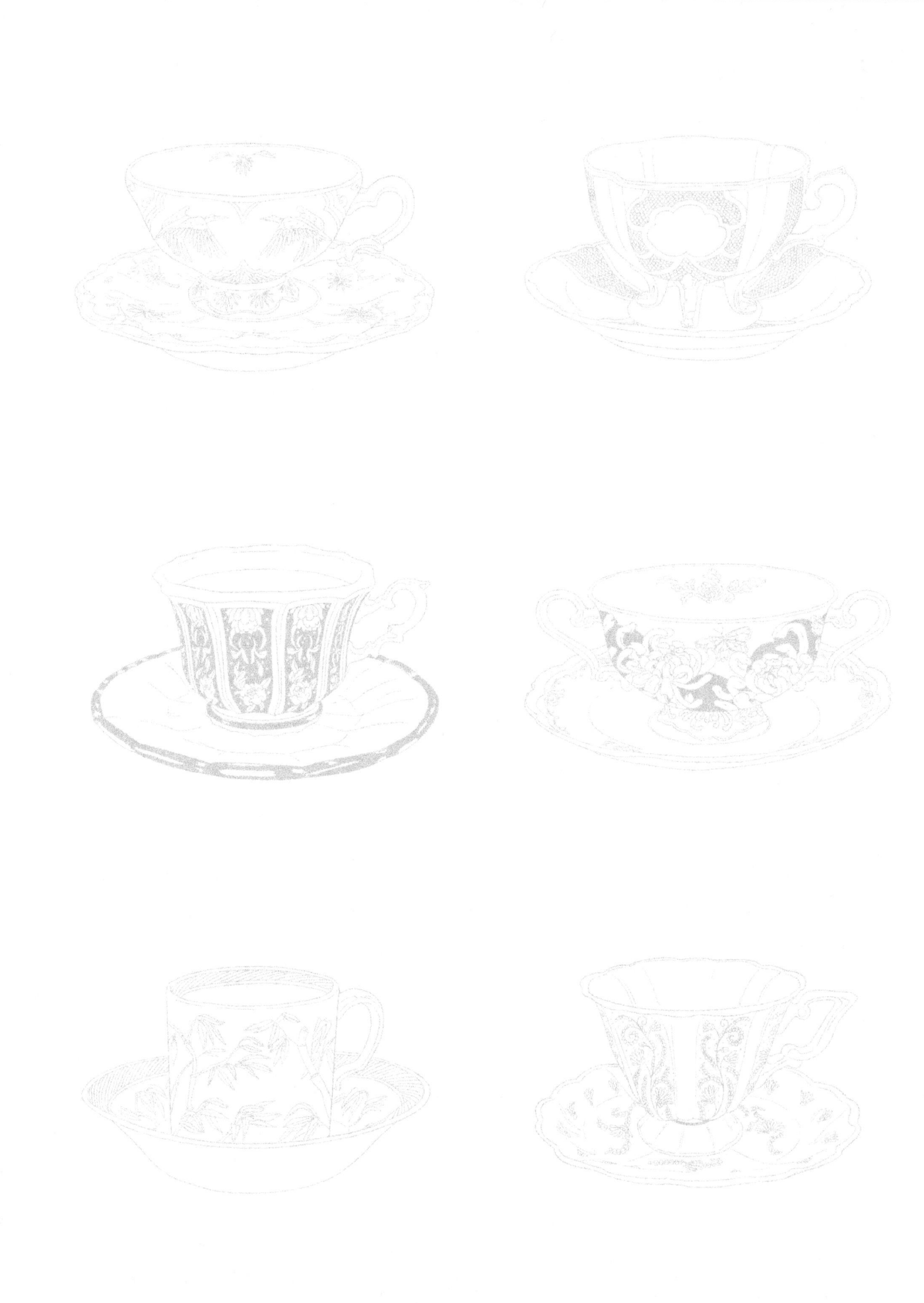

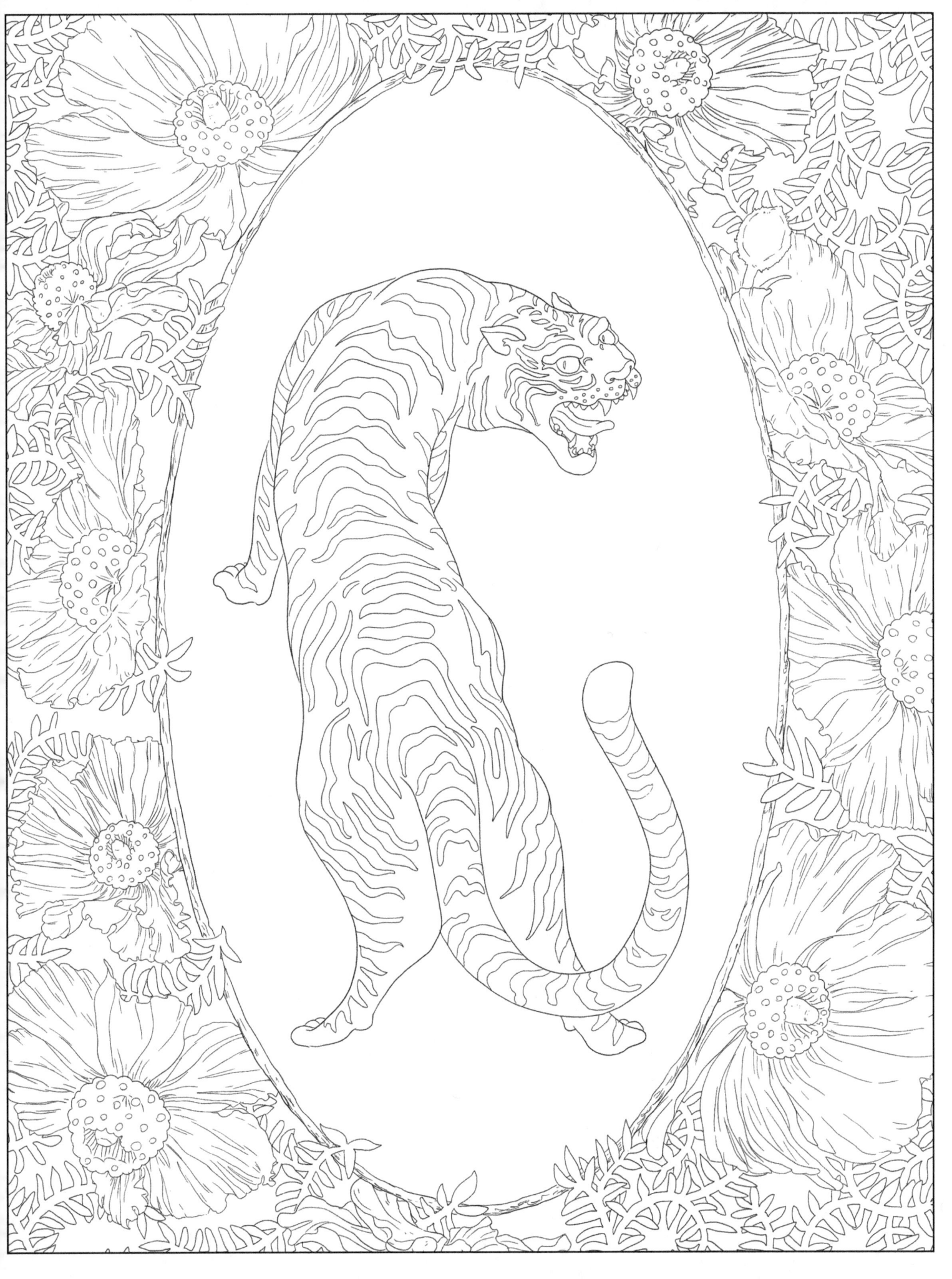

CHEEKY TIGER

CHEEKY TIGER

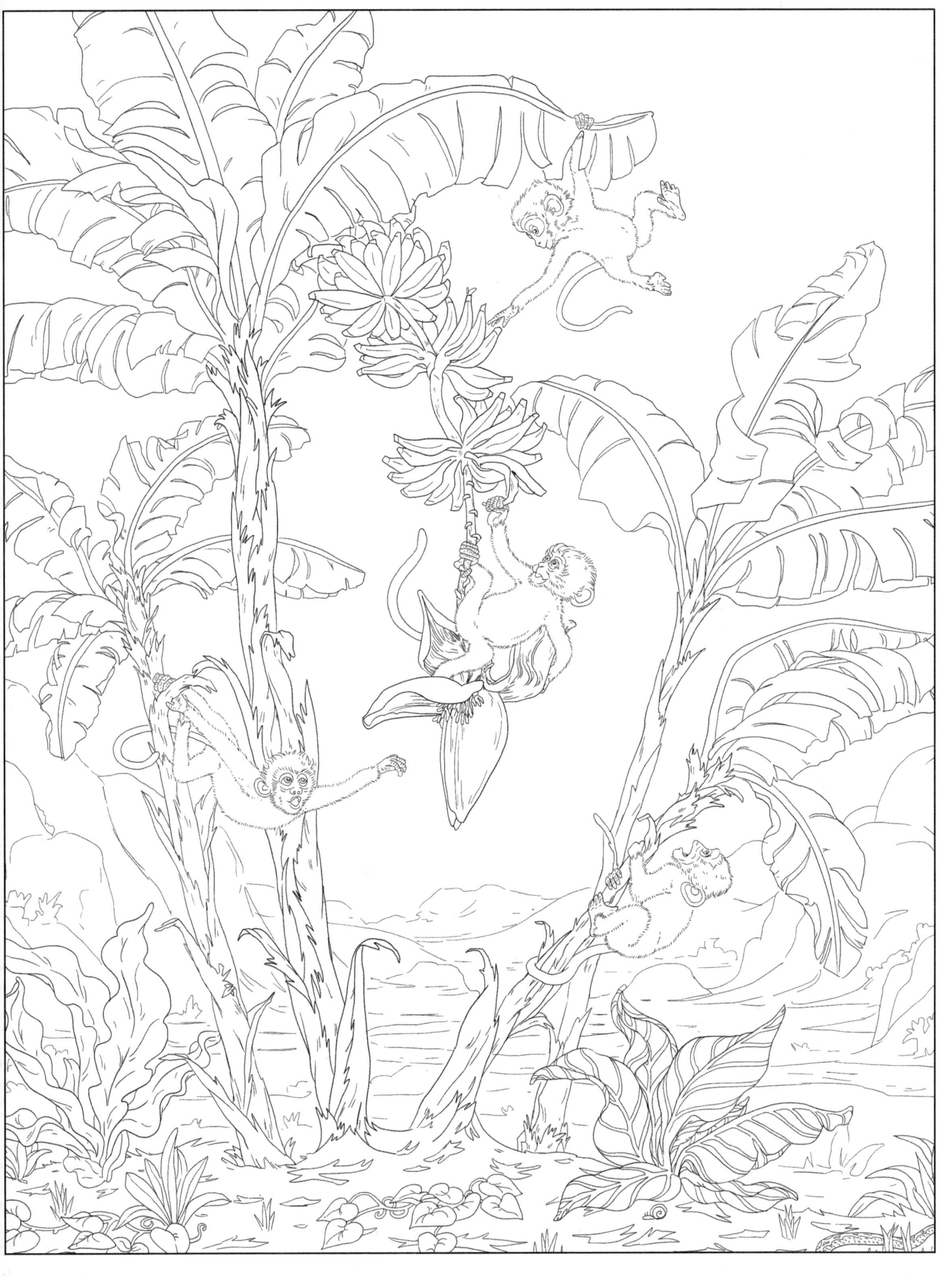

CHEEKIER MONKEYS

CHEEKIER MONKEYS

NEGATIVE RAM

NEGATIVE RAM

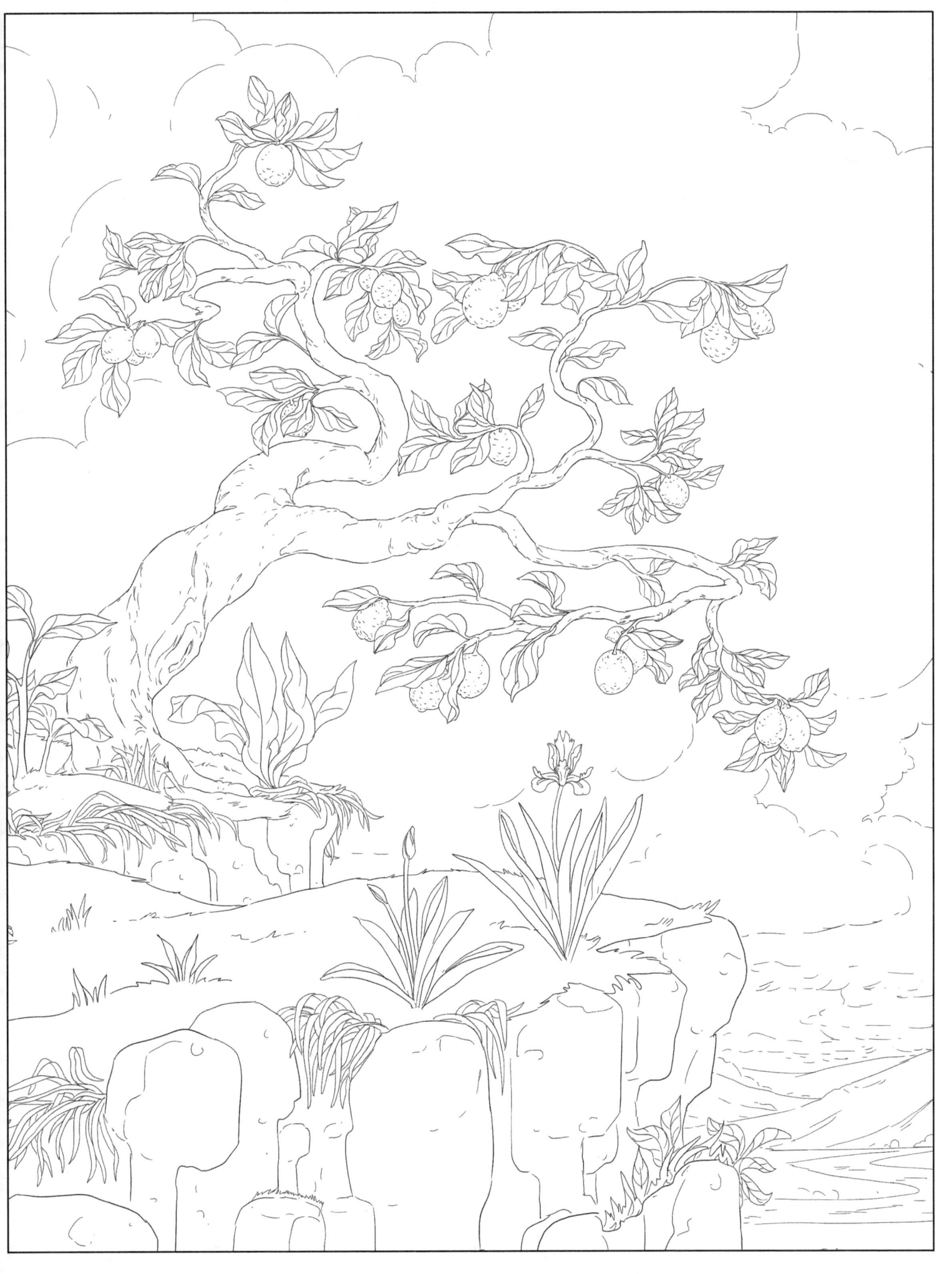

LEMON'S BLUFF

LEMON'S BLUFF

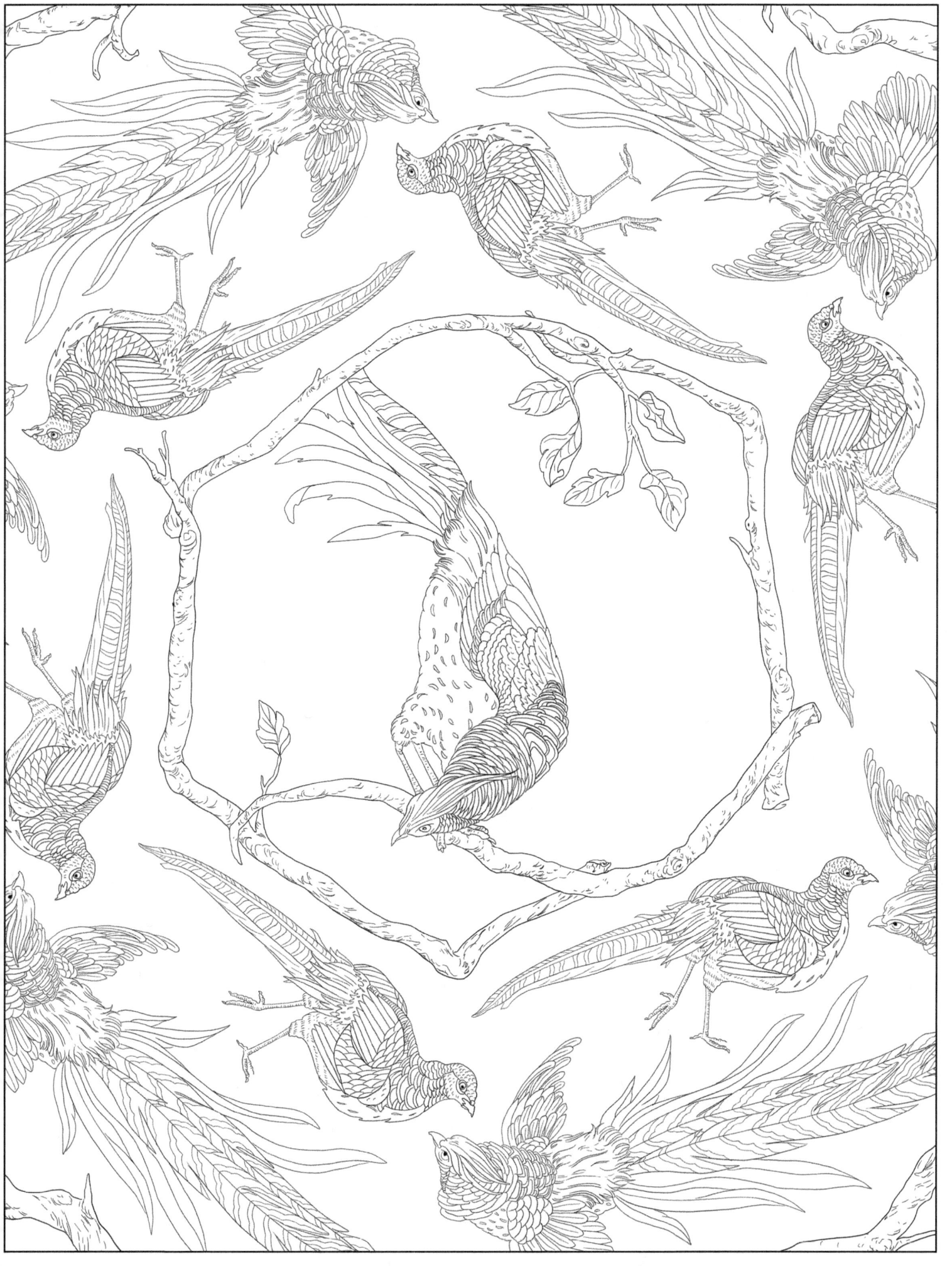

EXCESSIVE PHEASANTS

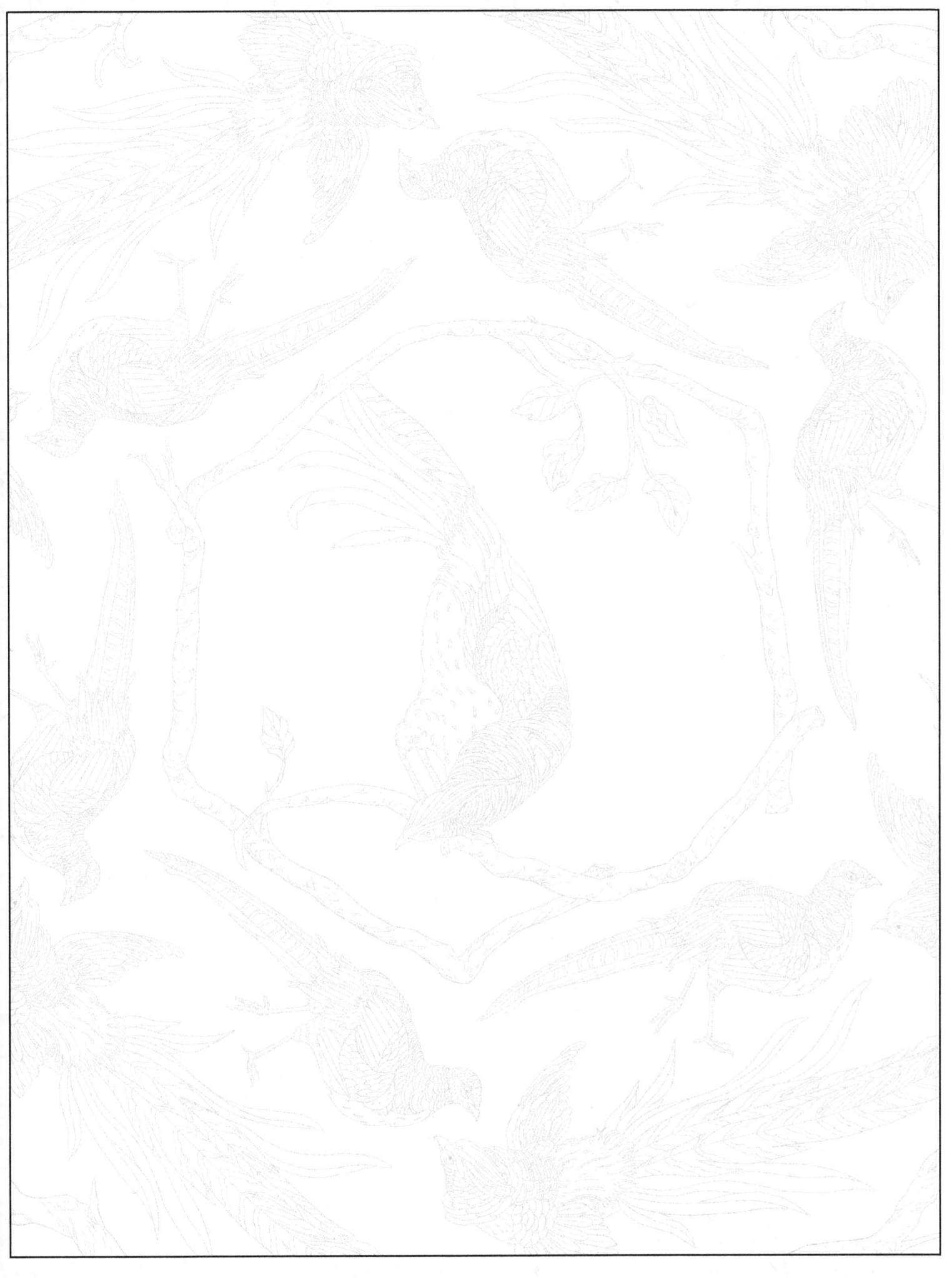

EXCESSIVE PHEASANTS

PEONY BRANCHES

PEONY BRANCHES

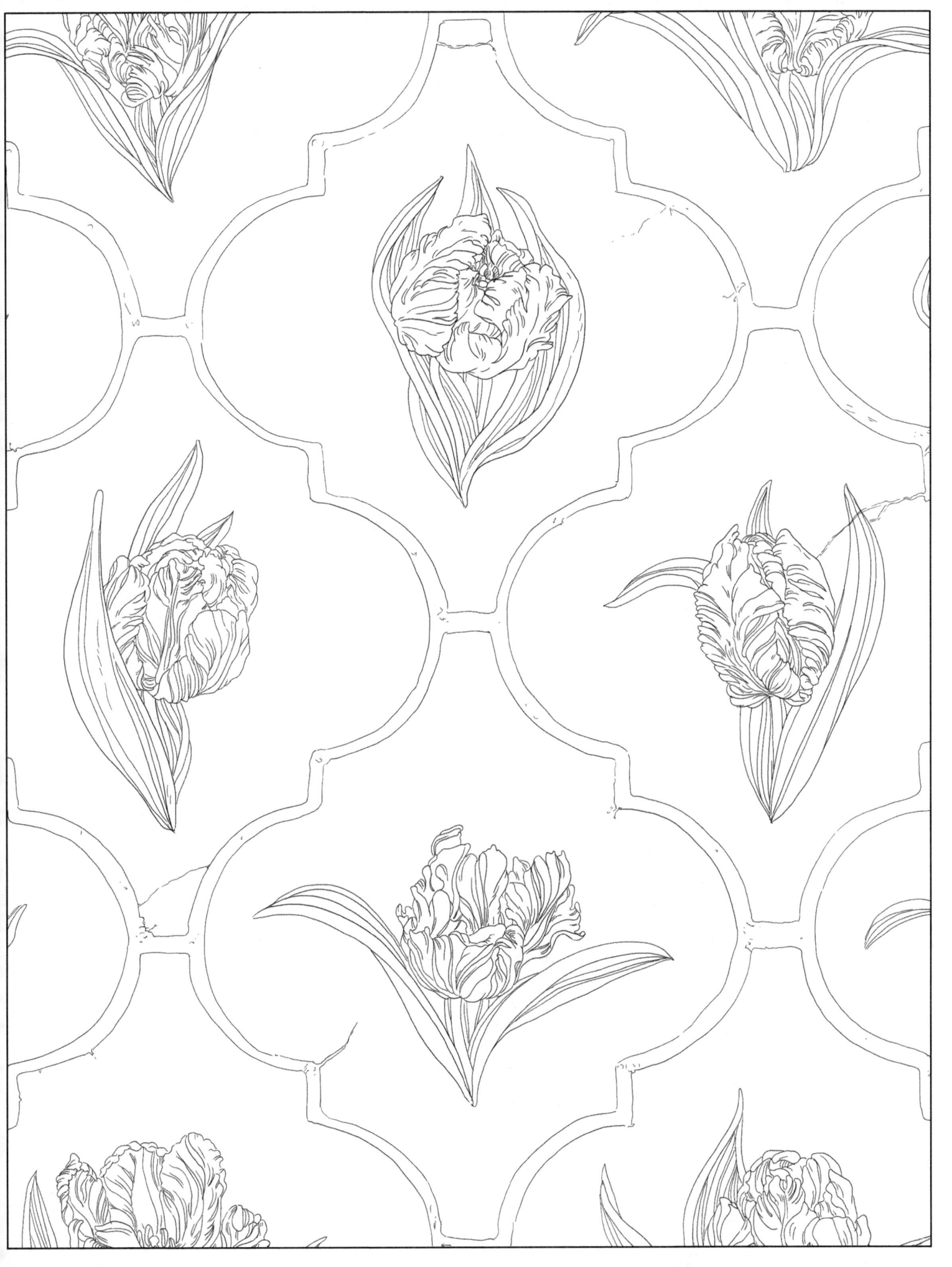

ARABESQUE TILES

ARABESQUE TILES

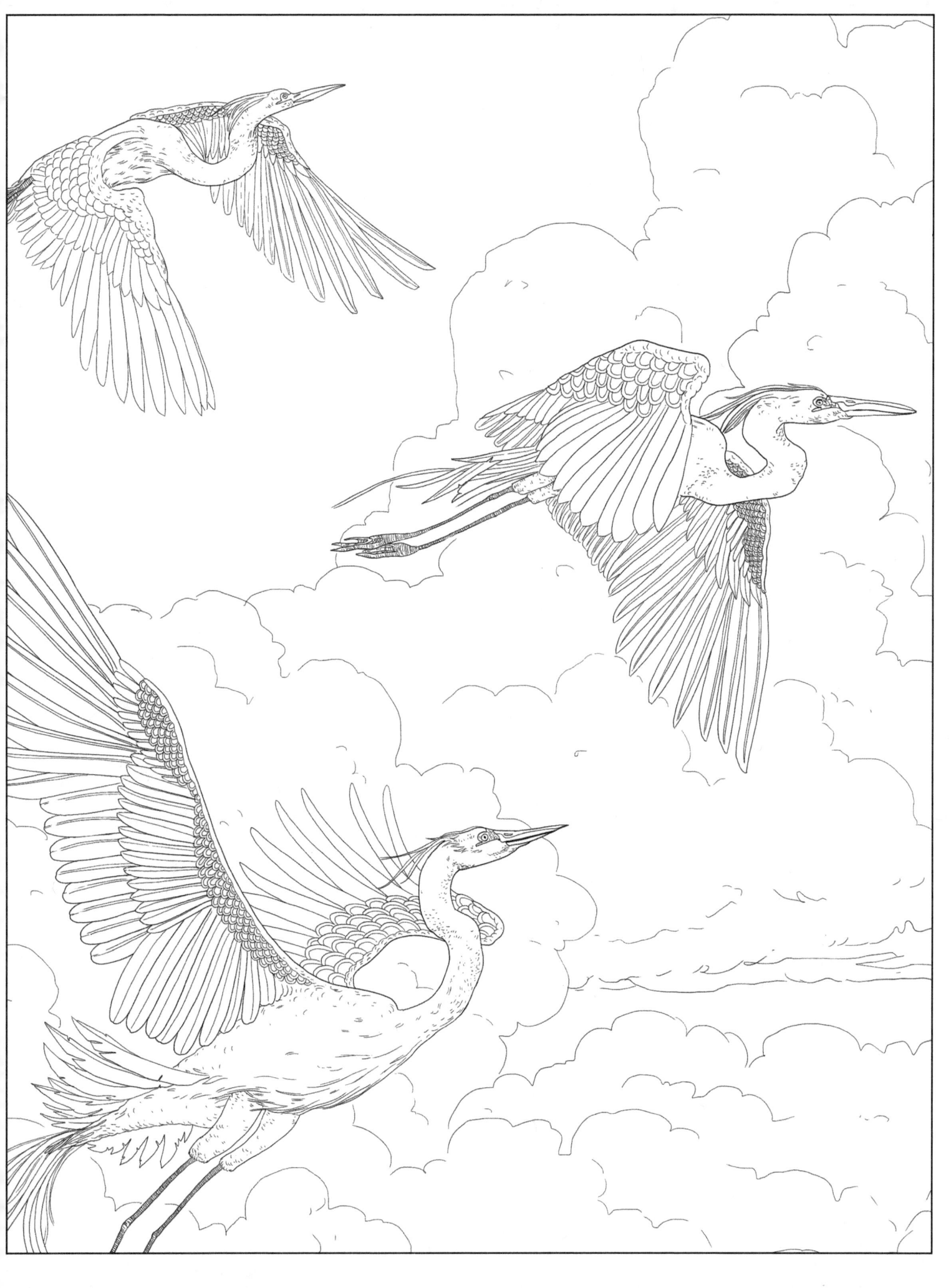

EGRETS AU REVOIR

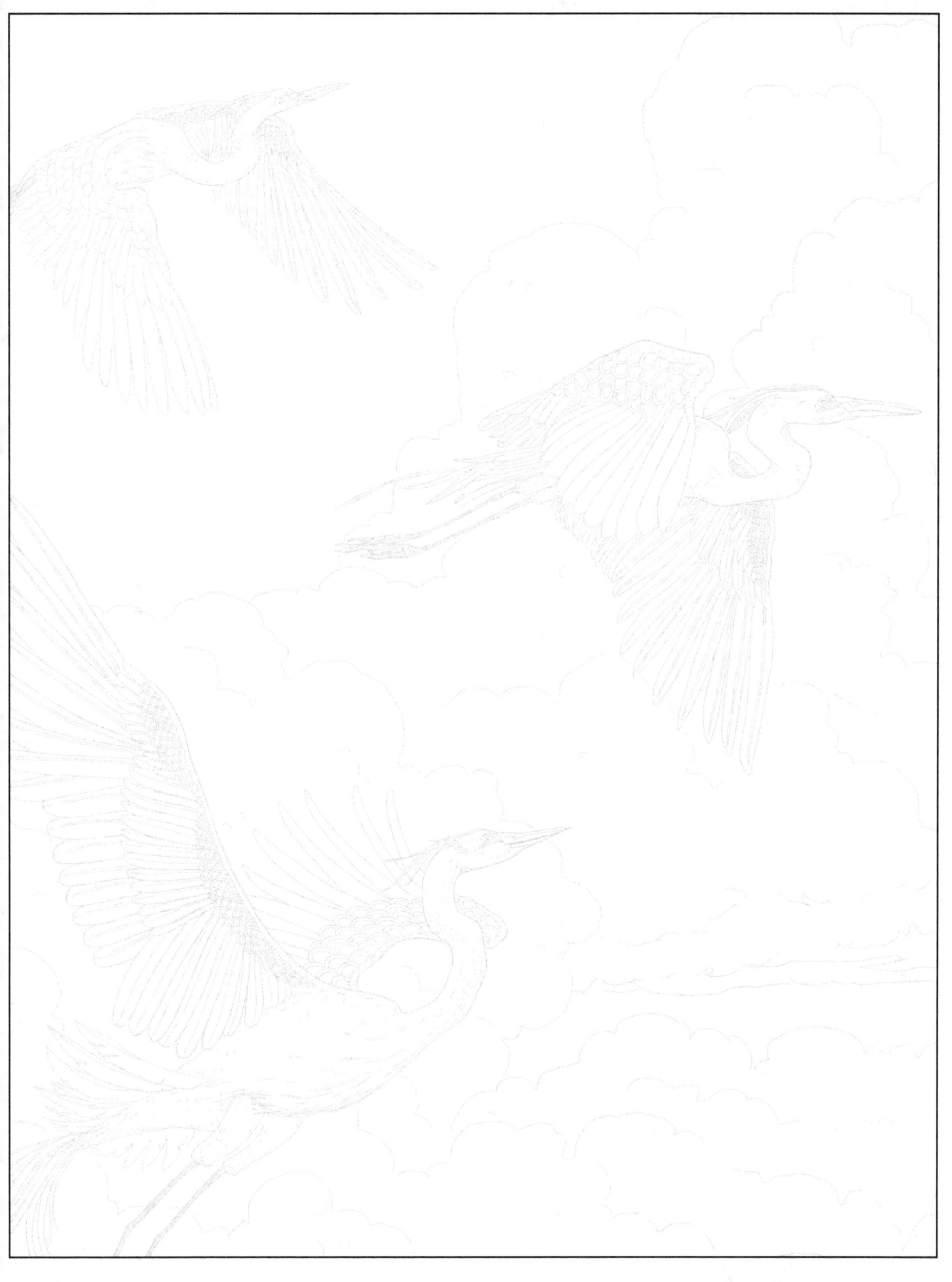

EGRETS AU REVOIR

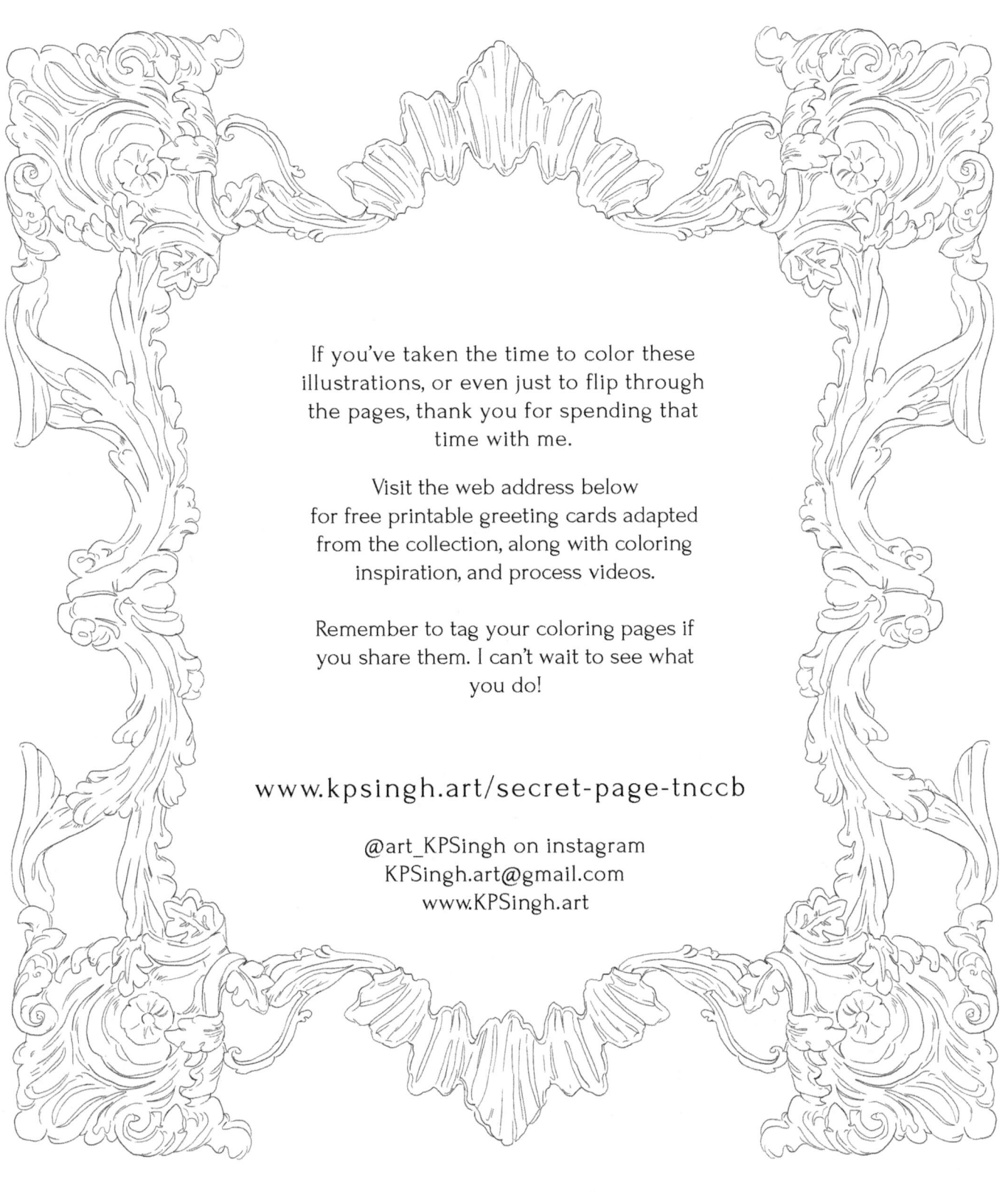

If you've taken the time to color these illustrations, or even just to flip through the pages, thank you for spending that time with me.

Visit the web address below for free printable greeting cards adapted from the collection, along with coloring inspiration, and process videos.

Remember to tag your coloring pages if you share them. I can't wait to see what you do!

www.kpsingh.art/secret-page-tnccb

@art_KPSingh on instagram
KPSingh.art@gmail.com
www.KPSingh.art

www.ingramcontent.com/pod-product-compliance
Lightning Source LLC
Chambersburg PA
CBHW082110220526
45472CB00009B/2119